Unsafety, Uncertainty, and Risk in Appeals Against Conviction in the Court of Appeal Criminal Division

This book examines the decision-making of the Court of Appeal, Criminal Division, of England and Wales in appeals against conviction through the lens of risk. This is achieved by normative evaluation of the concept of risk and how it is tolerated within the wider criminal justice system, and the implications of that tolerance for the Court of Appeal. This analysis involves consideration of recent Court decisions to further our understanding of its decision-making process, to advance the normative framework in this context, and to provide empirical support for the arguments presented. Ultimately the book argues that since the risk of injustice is tolerated elsewhere, there must exist a residual tolerance for injustice in the appeal system. The work makes a significant theoretical contribution to discourse on criminal appeals by linking the unsafety test to the general problem of uncertainty and risk taking. By doing so, it offers an insightful take on the purposes of criminal appeals and addresses concerns about decision-making in the Court of Appeal. The study will be of interest to academics, researchers, and practitioners working in the areas of criminal law and justice, studies related to miscarriages of justice, judicial decision-making, and criminology.

Paul Dargue is an assistant professor at Northumbria University School of Law, Northumbria University, UK. His research interests are in criminal law, criminal evidence, the criminal appeal system, and public law.

Routledge Studies in Courts and Legal Systems

Series Editor:

Nicola Monaghan *is a Principal Lecturer in Law at the University of Worcester, UK. Her research interests include jury misconduct, evidence and the criminal trial. She is an unregistered barrister and a member of the Honourable Society of the Middle Temple.*

This series covers aspects relating to courts in civil and criminal proceedings, and appellate courts and judges, in both domestic and international settings. It explores the role of courts, the role of actors within a court – including, lawyers, judges, court staff, expert witnesses, defendants, victims, and the jury – and the interplay between courts, the law, and the wider legal system. The series explores a variety of aspects relating to legal systems, the comparative differences in legal systems, and the role of courts and law within them.

Contributions that take either a comparative or single jurisdiction approach are welcomed, as are submissions for monographs or edited collections that address the civil law tradition or common law system. We actively encourage proposals from authors based in the Global South. Submissions which cover themes such as digital justice, the role of artificial intelligence and the courts, or alternative dispute resolution would also be very relevant.

Titles in this series:

Unsafety, Uncertainty, and Risk in Appeals Against Conviction in the Court of Appeal Criminal Division
Paul Dargue

Unsafety, Uncertainty, and Risk in Appeals Against Conviction in the Court of Appeal Criminal Division

Paul Dargue

Routledge
Taylor & Francis Group
LONDON AND NEW YORK

First published 2027
by Routledge
4 Park Square, Milton Park, Abingdon, Oxon OX14 4RN

and by Routledge
605 Third Avenue, New York, NY 10158

Routledge is an imprint of the Taylor & Francis Group, an informa business

British Library Cataloguing-in-Publication Data
A catalogue record for this book is available from the British Library

ISBN: 978-1-041-32132-3 (hbk)
ISBN: 978-1-041-32134-7 (pbk)
ISBN: 978-1-003-78229-2 (ebk)

DOI: 10.4324/9781003782292

Typeset in Times New Roman
by Apex CoVantage, LLC

To my family.

Contents

Introduction

Introduction

This book is a study of the approach of the England and Wales Court of Appeal (Criminal Division) (hereafter: 'the Court') in appeals against conviction. Since the enactment of the Criminal Appeal Act 1995, the Court has been required to allow appeals, and so quash the conviction(s) subject to appeal, if it thinks the conviction is 'unsafe'. The criminal appeal system, including the Court, is currently under review by the Law Commission and so there is a realistic prospect of legislative reform to its powers in the future. The core argument of this book is that the Court is required to protect appellants from the unacceptable risk of injustice, but not from all risk. The concept of risk, and the assessment and tolerance thereof, provides the optimal lens through which to understand from how much risk appellants ought to be protected, and to establish the extent and limits of the Court's role. The application of the lens of risk to the unsafety test in the context of criminal appeals offers a novel, timely, and innovative perspective of the Court's decision-making under conditions that are intrinsically uncertain. This chapter sets the scene for the argument to be made in the chapters that follow.

The Court of Appeal (Criminal Division)

This book is a study of the England and Wales Court of Appeal (Criminal Division) and its approach towards its powers in appeals against conviction. The Court hears appeals against conviction (in addition to other matters) on indictment.[1] Section 2 of the Criminal Appeal Act 1968, as amended by the Criminal Appeal Act 1995, states that the Court:

> 2(1)(a) shall allow an appeal against conviction if they think that the conviction is unsafe; and

1 Those other matters including appeals against sentence, interlocutory appeals, and appeals against allegedly unduly lenient sentences. This book is concerned only with appeals against conviction.

DOI: 10.4324/9781003782292-1

(b) shall dismiss such an appeal in any other case.

(2) In the case of an appeal against conviction the Court shall, if they allow the appeal, quash the conviction.

Section 2(1)(a) of the 1968 Act, as amended, refers to the question of whether the conviction 'is unsafe'; as such, it shall be referred to as the 'unsafety test' throughout this book. Any unsafe convictions must be quashed and replaced by an acquittal (subject to any retrial).[2] If the Court finds that the conviction is safe the appeal must be dismissed and the conviction will be upheld. The Court has a number of subsidiary powers, including to order a retrial (section 7), and to receive 'fresh evidence' (section 23).

Research has shown that the great majority of appeals concern procedural irregularities occurring before, during, or after trial.[3] Such irregularities can range from allegations that the trial was an abuse of process or unfair, some alleged mistake by the trial judge, issues with the trial judge's summing up, incompetent representation, police misconduct, irregularities relating to the jury, and so on.[4] These are also the most frequently successful grounds of appeal.[5] Fresh evidence is adduced comparatively less often by appellants, no doubt due to the difficulty in locating such evidence within the 28 days allowed to submit an application to appeal against conviction.[6] These are the primary kinds of appeal that appear before the Court, but there is a third kind often referred to as 'lurking doubt'. The phrase comes from the case of *Cooper*,[7] and the question is whether, despite there being no irregularity or fresh evidence, the Court has some lurking doubt that an injustice might have been done. This ground is rarely argued directly in Court,[8] and the Court does not encourage its use.[9]

The 1995 Act also created the Criminal Cases Review Commission (CCRC). It can refer cases to the Court of Appeal if it thinks there is a 'real possibility' the Court will find the conviction unsafe.[10] Since the CCRC started its work

2 Criminal Appeal Act 1968, s 7.

3 See K Malleson, 'Appeals against Conviction and the Principle of Finality' (1994) 21 (1) *Journal of Law and Society* 151; S Roberts, 'Fresh Evidence and Factual Innocence in the Criminal Division of the Court of Appeal' (2017) 81 (4) *Journal of Criminal Law* 303; P Dargue, 'The Tolerability of Risk in the Court of Appeal (Criminal Division): An Empirical Study of Appeals against Conviction 2015–2021' (2025) *Criminal Law Review* 743.

4 Examples of irregularities that can be argued at appeal are provided in practitioner texts such as P Taylor, *Taylor on Criminal Appeals* (3rd edn, Oxford University Press, 2022).

5 See Dargue (n 3).

6 See N Sakande, N Padfield, 'Time to Appeal: An Argument for Extending Time Limits' (2020) 10 *Criminal Law Review* 931.

7 *R v Cooper* [1969] 1 QB 267.

8 See Dargue (n 3).

9 In *R v Pope* [2012] EWCA Crim 2241. Discussed in more detail in chapter 1.

10 Criminal Appeal Act 1995, s 13.

in 1997, it has received more than 34,000 applications, has completed 33,000 reviews (including those that were ineligible), and referred 911 appeals back to the Court of Appeal, of which 613 have been allowed and 241 dismissed.[11] On any view, the prospects of having a case referred by the CCRC to the Court of Appeal are remote, and it has received significant criticism about its referral rates and institutional decision-making.[12] The CCRC as an institution is not the focus of this book and little more will be said about it directly.

The Court of Appeal's 'cautious' approach

In July 2022 the Law Commission was asked by the then-government to conduct a review of the law relating to criminal appeals, especially the decision-making of the Court of Appeal and the CCRC.[13] It published an issues paper in July 2023[14] and a consultation paper in July 2025.[15] The final report is expected in 2026, following which there is the possibility of legislative reform. Its terms of reference are to consider the need for reform of the law with a view to ensuring that the courts have powers that enable the 'effective, efficient and appropriate' resolution of appeals.[16] The Commission was asked to report on whether the test for allowing an appeal against conviction '*may hinder the correction of miscarriages of justice*'.[17] Furthermore, it was asked specifically to consider the Court's approach towards the unsafety test and the fresh evidence provisions.[18]

While the Court of Appeal is a creature of the various Criminal Appeal Acts, it exists as part of the broader criminal justice system and so is subject to the general norms of the criminal justice system and the Criminal Procedure Rules. The Rules provide that any court dealing with a criminal case must further the overriding objective when exercising any power given to it by legislation.[19] The overriding objective is to *deal with cases justly*.[20] Dealing with cases justly includes acquitting the innocent, convicting the guilty, dealing with the prosecution and defence fairly, observing the defendant's fair trial

11 See CCRC, https://ccrc.gov.uk/facts-figures/. The remainder are outstanding at the time of writing.
12 A detailed study of the CCRC as an institution can be found in C Hoyle, M Sato, *Reasons to Doubt: Wrongful Convictions and the Criminal Cases Review Commission* (Oxford University Press, 2019).
13 See the consultation website: https://lawcom.gov.uk/project/criminal-appeals/
14 Law Commission, *Criminal Appeals: Issues Paper* (Law Commission, 2023).
15 Law Commission, *Criminal Appeals: Consultation Paper* (Law Comm No 268, 2025) [1.4].
16 Law Commission, *Criminal Appeals: Consultation Paper* (Law Comm No 268, 2025) [1.5].
17 Law Commission, *Criminal Appeals: Consultation Paper* (Law Comm No 268, 2025) [1.5].
18 Law Commission, *Criminal Appeals: Consultation Paper* (Law Comm No 268, 2025) [1.5].
19 Criminal Procedure Rules r1.3(a).
20 Rules (n 19) r1.1(1).

rights, acting efficiently, and proportionally, and expeditiously.[21] All of these aspects are important components of justice in their own right, but getting the facts right – acquitting the innocent and convicting the guilty – is of particular importance.

The Court of Appeal holds the crucial role within the criminal justice system of being able to quash convictions to ultimately deal with cases justly. Quashing a conviction is not something that is to be taken lightly; considerable resources are expended in procuring convictions, in order to secure the social good of convicting the guilty. The tool the Court has been given is the unsafety test and the jurisprudence based upon it; its approach towards the crucial boundary between safety and unsafety is central. In the House of Lords case of *Pendleton*,[22] thus binding on the Court of Appeal, Lord Bingham[23] said that the Court's power to quash convictions is a power 'to be exercised with caution, mindful that the Court of Appeal is not privy to the jury's deliberations and must not intrude into territory which properly belongs to the jury'.[24]

Thus, the Court would describe its approach as 'cautious'. It is not easy to have an appeal against conviction allowed; roughly one-in-twenty of those that apply for permission to appeal are ultimately successful.[25] The criminal process is long and expensive, during which all parts of the wider system were also trying to deal with the case justly, especially getting the facts right by acquitting the innocent and convicting the guilty. Most appeals before the Court of Appeal are generated by contested Crown Court trials, and so it was usually a jury which decided that the appellant is guilty.[26] Consequently, if all the evidence was heard by the jury, the trial judge appropriately directed them, and there were no significant legal irregularities that could impact their verdict, the appellant is unlikely to have any appeal against conviction allowed.[27] The Court would describe its approach as 'cautious'. However, is it *too* cautious? Is it in fact not merely 'cautious', but 'unduly cautious' to allow appeals?

There is a wide body of literature which maintains that this is the case.[28] This book challenges the supposition that the Court's approach is unduly cautious. It

21 Rules (n 19) r1.1(2)(a – h).

22 [2001] UKHL 66.

23 Lord Bingham was Lord Chief Justice around the enactment of the Criminal Appeal Act 1995, and so made several important decisions on the meaning of unsafety in the context of criminal appeals.

24 *R v Pendelton* (n 22) 17.

25 See Court of Appeal, *Annual Reports 2023–2024*, https://www.judiciary.uk/guidance-and-resources/a-review-of-the-year-in-the-court-of-appeal-criminal-division-october-2023-september-2024/ annex D.

26 The exceptions being where the appellant pleaded guilty, and rarer-still cases where an appellant was convicted in a trial by judge alone.

27 There is a long line of empirical research demonstrating this; see Dargue (n 3).

28 See e.g. M Knight, *Criminal Appeals* (Stephen and Sons, 1970); C Walker, K Starmer (eds), *Justice in Error* (Blackstone, 1993); R Pattenden, *English Criminal Appeals 1844–1994* (Clarendon

does so by situating the function of the Court within the framework of risk, and the assessment and toleration therefore.

A risk based approach

This book offers a novel and timely conceptual and empirical re-appraisal of the supposition that the Court's approach is unduly narrow. The unsafety test is a nebulous and inchoate power, designed to give the Court maximum flexibility. The idea that the Court is in some general sense unduly cautious is, therefore, too slippery a supposition to be a useful basis for reform. Accordingly, a surer theoretical framework is required. The concept of risk, and the assessment and tolerance thereof, is a more useful and substantive concept and provides an optimal lens through which to study the Court's decision-making. Unlike the concept of having a general 'narrow approach', it is understood what taking a risk means. By applying the concept of risk to criminal appeals, there can be a conceptual foundation and a baseline of what the Court should do and should not do.

The argument made in this book is as follows. The unsafety test is exercised under conditions of uncertainty and so is a risk taking activity. In ordinary life, risks are generally assessed by assessment of the severity of the harm risked and the likelihood of that harm occurring.[29] In safety management terms: a situation is safe when there is '*freedom from unacceptable risk*', and unsafety is the opposite.[30] As such, achieving safety does not ordinarily require the extinguishing of all risk, but its reduction to an acceptable level. Risks should be as low as reasonably practicable (ALARP), not reduced more than is reasonable.

The Court does not talk in terms of risk, but it does talk in terms of safety and unsafety. Since something is safe when there is freedom from unacceptable risk, risk as a concept maps onto the unsafety test to supply a theoretical framework for study of the Court. The function of the Court of Appeal is, therefore, to protect appellants from the unacceptable risk of injustice; it is not its function to protect from all risk. The Court must instead assess how much risk of injustice can be tolerated and decide whether it needs to act to protect the appellant from that risk. This framework, it is argued, provides a conceptual baseline of protection that is currently absent.

Press, 1996); R Nobles, D Schiff, *Understanding Miscarriages of Justice: The Law, the Media, and the Inevitability of Crisis* (Oxford University Press, 2000); M Naughton, *The Innocent and the Criminal Justice System: A Sociological Analysis of Miscarriages of Justice* (Palgrave MacMillan, 2013).

29 See M Marletta, 'Probabilities, Cost, and Justice: Rethinking Precautionary Measures in Civil and Criminal Law' (2025) 24 *Law, Probability, and Risk* 1.

30 Eg H A Oltedal, 'Setting the Scene for Maritime Safety Management' in A Oltedal, M Lützhöft (eds), *Managing Maritime Safety* (Routledge, 2018) 7; E Hollnagel, *Safety-II in Practice: Developing the Resilience Potentials* (CRC Press, 2017) 22.

Criminal appeals 2024

In addition to the development of this theoretical framework, this study introduces new empirical evidence to support this argument, namely qualitative analysis of a sample of the Court of Appeal's decisions handed down in 2024. The sample employed in Chapter 3 is of 101 appeals against conviction and 195 renewed applications for permission to appeal, a total of 296 cases. The appeals are analysed in a qualitative manner through the lens of risk in order to assess whether the Court does protect appellants from unacceptable risk.

The analysis of the Court's judgments demonstrates that most appeals against conviction involve routine questions, usually regarding the application of discrete questions of law. When the Court's decision-making is seen as requiring the assessment of risk, it is impossible to say that the Court does not in general adequately protect appellants. Claims to the contrary are, therefore, overblown and lack a sense of reality regarding the Court's routine decision-making. That said, there are certain aspects of its decision-making where the Court could take a more protective role.

The structure of this book

This book contains four chapters. Chapter 1 explains the provenance and meaning of the unsafety test in the context of criminal appeals. It includes a detailed explanation of the purposes, procedures, and workload of the Court Appeal, and detailed exposition of the operation of the unsafety test in criminal appeals. As noted earlier, the Court of Appeal has sustained significant criticism for an allegedly unduly narrow approach. This view is presented and then critiqued. It is concluded that talk of a narrow approach (and so attempts to alter such an approach) ought to be abandoned in favour of assessment of the Court's tolerance of risk.

Chapter 2 turns to the assessment of risk. Appeals against conviction take place in conditions of uncertainty and so involve the taking of risk. A detailed explanation of the concept of risk, and the assessment and tolerance thereof, is provided so far as relevant to decision-making in the Court of Appeal. It is argued that the Court is required to assess the risks that are taken elsewhere in the criminal process – and in particular at the trial – in order to assess which of its own options are the least risky at light of its function to protect appellants from unacceptable risk. Some risk of unwanted outcome must be tolerable, and the Court is not required to reduce the risk more than reasonably practicable.

Chapter 3 presents the results of a qualitative study of the Court's decisions handed down in 2024 to demonstrate the Court's handling of risk. It is argued that the optimal lens through which to observe and scrutinise the Court's decision is the lens of risk assessment. Based upon the ordinary principles of risk and the premise that the Court's function is to protect appellants from unacceptable risk, the lens is applied to the Court's routine decision-making to examine whether the Court does comply with that standard. It is argued that on the whole the Court does comply, but observes some limitations with its decision-making, in particular in relation to fresh evidence. This is a novel and innovative study of the Court applying the concept of risk.

The fourth chapter scrutinises some of the reform proposals made by the Law Commission, and offers some of the author's own proposals for reform based around the theoretical framework of assessing risk. There is a realistic prospect of legislative reform to the Court's powers in the near future, and it is crucial that reform is clearly directed towards its function: to protect appellants from unacceptable risk. Chapter 4 makes innovative suggestions for reform to the Court's powers and processes that engage with this prospect of reform.

Conclusion

This book utilises the core concepts of risk assessment, risk tolerance, and risk management to conceptually and empirically critique the criminal appeal system of England and Wales. The way the appeal system is currently analysed, by reference to whether its approach is narrow or restrictive, is inappropriate and not useful, especially when legislative reform might be considered in the future. The concept of risk provides a more substantive and useful lens through which to observe the appeal system and the decision-making of the Court of Appeal. It is argued that when the Court's decision-making is understood as an example of decision-making under conditions of uncertainty, it becomes clear that its core function is to protect appellants from the unacceptable risks of injustice. With this framework in place, this book offers an original and significant contribution to the analysis of the criminal appeal system at an important time in light of proposals for reform.

References

CCRC, https://ccrc.gov.uk/facts-figures/

Court of Appeal, *Annual Reports 2023–2024*, https://www.judiciary.uk/guidance-and-resources/a-review-of-the-year-in-the-court-of-appeal-criminal-division-october-2023-september-2024/

Criminal Appeal Act 1968

Criminal Procedure Rules

Dargue, P, 'The Tolerability of Risk in the Court of Appeal (Criminal Division): An Empirical Study of Appeals against Conviction 2015–2021' (2025) *Criminal Law Review* 743

Hollnagel, E, *Safety-II in Practice: Developing the Resilience Potentials* (CRC Press, 2017)

Hoyle, C, Sato, M, *Reasons to Doubt: Wrongful Convictions and the Criminal Cases Review Commission* (Oxford University Press, 2019)

Knight, M, *Criminal Appeals* (Stephen and Sons, 1970)

Law Commission, *Criminal Appeals: Consultation Paper* (Law Comm No 268, 2025)
Law Commission, *Criminal Appeals: Issues Paper* (Law Commission, 2023)
Malleson, K, 'Appeals against Conviction and the Principle of Finality' (1994) 21 (1) *Journal of Law and Society* 151
Marletta, M, 'Probabilities, Cost, and Justice: Rethinking Precautionary Measures in Civil and Criminal Law' (2025) 24 *Law, Probability, and Risk* 1
Naughton, M, *The Innocent and the Criminal Justice System: A Sociological Analysis of Miscarriages of Justice* (Palgrave MacMillan, 2013)
Nobles, R, Schiff, D, *Understanding Miscarriages of Justice: The Law, The Media, and the Inevitability of Crisis* (Oxford University Press, 2000)
Oltedal, H A, 'Setting the Scene for Maritime Safety Management' in Oltedal, H A, Lützhöft, M, (eds), *Managing Maritime Safety* (Routledge, 2018) 7
Pattenden, R, *English Criminal Appeals 1844–1994* (Clarendon Press, 1996)
R v Cooper [1969] 1 QB 267
R v Pendleton [2001] UKHL 66
R v Pope [2012] EWCA Crim 2241
Roberts, S, 'Fresh Evidence and Factual Innocence in the Criminal Division of the Court of Appeal' (2017) 81 (4) *Journal of Criminal Law* 30
Sakande, N, Padfield, N, 'Time to Appeal: An Argument for Extending Time Limits' (2020) 10 *Criminal Law Review* 931
Taylor, P, *Taylor on Criminal Appeals* (3rd edn, Oxford University Press, 2022)
Walker, C, Starmer, K, (eds), *Justice in Error* (Blackstone, 1993)

1 The England and Wales Court of Appeal (Criminal Division)

Introduction

In order to understand the present study of the Court's approach through the lens of risk, it is necessary to understand the purposes of the appeal system, its procedures, and its workload. The Court has exercised the unsafety test since the enactment of the Criminal Appeal Act 1995; this chapter provides a detailed exposition of that test in practice. The unsafety test is a product of its history, and as such, to properly understand the unsafety test, it is beneficial to consider some of that history. While the Court is required to exercise the unsafety test, it forms part of the criminal justice system and so is compelled to deal with cases justly. To that end, the Court has faced sustained criticism that it may fail to do so due to an overly reluctant approach towards quashing convictions. That view is presented and then critiqued. It is ultimately argued that there are limitations with that view, and that view should be abandoned in favour of a conception of the unsafety test centred around risk.

The England and Wales Court of Appeal (Criminal Division)

Purpose

The England and Wales Court of Appeal (Criminal Division) is housed in the Royal Courts of Justice, London. It is staffed by judges who have reached close to the pinnacle of the legal profession in England and Wales: lawyers who demonstrate 'graft, quick-thinking, genius, and stamina'.[1] It is headed by the Lord or Lady Chief Justice of England and Wales (currently Lady Carr), assisted by the Vice President of the Court of Appeal (Criminal Division) (currently Edis LJ), and the President of the King's Bench Division of the

1 P Darbyshire, *Sitting in Judgment: The Working Lives of Judges* (Hart, 2011) 323–328.

DOI: 10.4324/9781003782292-2

High Court (currently Dame Victoria Sharp). Its judicial staff includes a cast of Lords and Ladies Justice of Appeal, High Court judges, senior circuit judges and recorders, and retired members thereof. It hears appeals against conviction on indictment, as well as other matters. As such, most of the appeals that appear before the Court are generated by contested Crown Court jury trials.

In his *Review of the Criminal Courts*, Sir Robin Auld (a former judge of the Court of Appeal) said that the primary purposes of appeal courts are to do justice in individual cases by correcting wrong decisions, and to engender public confidence in the administration of justice.[2] With these purposes in mind, the main criteria of a good criminal appeal system is one that does justice to defendants and the prosecution, brings finality, and is accessible, clear, efficient, and speedy.[3] Auld's recommendations for the codification of criminal law, criminal procedure, and sentencing[4] led to the Courts Act 2003, which created the Criminal Procedure Rules Committee.[5] The first set of Criminal Procedure Rules were drafted in 2005, with the most recent amendments in 2025.[6] The Criminal Procedure Rules provide that the 'overriding objective' is to *deal with cases justly.* Rule 1.1(2) provides that dealing with cases justly includes (inter alia) doing the following:

(a) acquitting the innocent and convicting the guilty
(b) treating all participants with politeness and respect
(c) dealing with the prosecution and the defence fairly
(d) recognising the rights of a defendant, particularly those under Article 6 of the European Convention on Human Rights.

Rule 1.2 states that anyone involved in any way with a criminal case is required to prepare and conduct the case in accordance with the overriding objective. By rule 1.3 courts must further the overriding objective when exercising any power or applying or interpreting any rule or practice direction. For the avoidance of doubt, this includes any appellants and lawyers appearing before the Court of Appeal, the Court of Appeal staff, and the judges of the Court. If the overriding objective is truly 'overriding', then the overriding duty of the Court of Appeal in any appeal against conviction is to deal with the case justly. The unsafety test, and its subsidiary powers (discussed in the following) are the tools the Court has been provided to satisfy that aim.

2 R Auld, *Review of the Criminal Courts of England and Wales* (HMSO, 2001) 611.
3 R Auld, *Review of the Criminal Courts of England and Wales* (HMSO, 2001) 611.
4 R Auld, *Review of the Criminal Courts of England and Wales* (HMSO, 2001) 23.
5 Courts Act 2003, s. 69.
6 See Criminal Procedure Rules, https://www.gov.uk/guidance/criminal-procedure-rules-2025-and-criminal-practice-directions-2023.

Section 2 of the 1968 Act was amended by the Criminal Appeal Act 1995. As amended, it reads that the judges of the Court:

> 2(1)(a) shall allow an appeal against conviction if they think that the conviction is unsafe; and
> (b) shall dismiss such an appeal in any other case.
> (2) In the case of an appeal against conviction the Court shall, if they allow the appeal, quash the conviction.

Allowing the appeal records an acquittal, unless a retrial is ordered. There is no indication of the meaning of the word 'unsafe' in the Act; it has been left to the judiciary to interpret. The test is broad enough to cover appellants who are innocent (i.e. victims of a miscarriage of justice) or possibly innocent, and appellants (whether guilty or not) who were convicted following lapses of due process or by a process hampered by procedural irregularity or unfairness (discussed in the following). Yet, the unsafety test requires the upholding of convictions if, but only if, the Court is satisfied the conviction is safe. This is the instruction it has received from Parliament; it must separate appellants' convictions into pools that are quashed and those that are upheld, and it must do so in the pursuit of justice. That means that doing what is thought to be in the interests of justice can require that some appeals are dismissed.

This creates a problem. Leaving things as they are could mean that wrongful convictions and miscarriages of justice might be left as they are. As Lord Bingham said, perpetuating such an injustice is repellent.[7] Wherever there is a prospect of dismissing an appeal against conviction an injustice could be done, but it would be unreasonable to expect perfection from the Court. How far is the Court expected to go to avoid perpetuating injustice? The Criminal Appeal Act is silent; it merely refers to quashing convictions that are unsafe. It is argued that the lens of risk helps to provide an answer to that question; the Court's function is to protect appellants from the unacceptable risk of injustice, but it need not go further. That view is sustained in the first two chapters of this book and applied in Chapter 3.

Other powers

The Court has a number of additional powers. Chief amongst those is the power to order a retrial whenever an appeal is allowed. The Court can order a retrial whenever it thinks it is in the interests of justice to do so.[8] The Court can, if it allows an appeal, substitute a conviction for another offence in

7 T Bingham, 'Justice and Injustice' in T Bingham (ed), *The Business of Judging* (Oxford University Press, 2000) 296.
8 Criminal Appeal Act 1968, ss 7–8.

certain circumstances.[9] If some convictions are quashed and some are upheld, the Court can re-sentence the appellant.[10] The Court can direct the Criminal Cases Review Commission (CCRC) to investigate and report on any matter it (the Court) thinks is relevant to the determination of an appeal.[11]

The fresh evidence provisions in section 23 of the Criminal Appeal Act 1968 (as amended) provide that the Court can receive evidence not adduced at trial if it thinks it thinks 'necessary and expedient in the interests of justice to do so' (section 23(1)). In deciding whether it is in the interests of justice to receive it, the Court must consider the following factors (section 23(2)):

> (a) whether the evidence appears to the Court to be capable of belief;
> (b) whether it appears to the Court that the evidence may afford any ground for allowing the appeal;
> (c) whether the evidence would have been admissible in the proceedings from which the appeal lies on an issue which is the subject of the appeal; and
> (d) whether there is a reasonable explanation for the failure to adduce the evidence in those proceedings.

The extent to which convictions can be upheld despite there being evidence that has not been assessed by a jury is one of the Court's major problem-areas, and is a recurring theme of this book.

The Court's workload

In the legal year ending September 2024 the Court received 1163 applications for permission to appeal, ultimately hearing 135 appeals, allowing 61 and dismissing 74.[12] It is worth noting that the number of persons applying for permission to appeal has been trending downwards for some time; for instance, in 2015–16, 1417 persons applied for permission, which declined to 1197 in 2017–18.[13] The Covid-19 pandemic accelerated that decline; applications for permission to appeal dropped as low as 800 per year between the years 2019–2022, before increasing again.[14] These numbers are not very revealing on their own, but demonstrate that on average an application for permission to appeal has a low prospect of progressing to an appeal, but once a case reaches the stage of having an appeal heard there is a better prospect of success.

9 Criminal Appeal Act 1968, s. 3.
10 Criminal Appeal Act 1968, s. 4.
11 Criminal Appeal Act 1968, s. 23A.
12 Court of Appeal, *Annual Report 2023–2024*, https://www.judiciary.uk/wp-content/uploads/2025/01/24.278_JO_A_Review_of_the_Year_In_the_Court_of_Appeal_Criminal_Division_2023-24_WEB.pdf
13 Court of Appeal, *Annual Report 2019–2020*, https://www.judiciary.uk/wp-content/uploads/2022/07/6.7429_JO_Court_of_Appeal_Criminalwillbet.pdf
14 Court of Appeal, *Annual Report 2022–2023*, https://www.judiciary.uk/wp-content/uploads/2024/07/24.16_JO_A_Review_of_the_Year_In_the_Court_of_Appeal_Criminal_Division_2022-23_WEB.pdf

It is generally considered that there are two kinds of appeals that appear before the Court with any regularity: appeals based on procedural irregularity and appeals based on fresh evidence, although appellants can and do rely on both at the same time. Subject to the need to obtain permission to appeal for each ground, there are no real constraints on the kinds of procedural irregularities an appellant can adduce. Any number of things can go wrong in the criminal process up to and including the trial, and any of these could be used to advance an appeal against conviction; it is thus impossible and unnecessary to list all the possible irregularities that can arise. The leading practitioner text, *Taylor on Criminal Appeals,* lists the most common irregularities.[15] There is a third kind of appeal – more of a concept – that is a contentious topic in the context of criminal appeals; that of 'lurking doubt' (discussed further in the following).

A quantitative study of 931 appeals against conviction between 2015 and 2021 affirmed previous findings regarding the Court's workload.[16] These results bear brief repetition to contextualise the Court's decision-making. Since the Court of Appeal hears appeals following conviction on indictment, it follows that the majority of the Court's workload concerns high-level offending. Some 24% of appeals concerned sexual offending; 16% were homicides, and 11% serious non-fatal offences of violence.[17] The study observed differences in success-rates for certain offences; for instance, homicide convictions were markedly less likely to be quashed than any other offences.[18]

It was found that 87% of appellants raised procedural irregularity grounds.[19] Procedural irregularities were accordingly the most frequently successful grounds of appeal.[20] The most commonly raised procedural grounds related to allegations of some defect in the trial judge's summing up, allegations that the trial judge wrongly admitted or excluded some piece of evidence, and allegations that the trial judge wrongly failed to accede to a submission of no case to answer.[21] Fresh evidence was raised in 13% of cases used in that study.[22] The study also found differences and nuances in the likelihood

15 P Taylor, *Taylor on Criminal Appeals* (3rd edn, Oxford University Press, 2022).

16 P Dargue, 'The Tolerability of Risk in the Court of Appeal (Criminal Division): An Empirical Study of Appeals against Conviction 2015–2021' (2025) *Criminal Law Review* 743.

17 P Dargue, 'The Tolerability of Risk in the Court of Appeal (Criminal Division): An Empirical Study of Appeals against Conviction 2015–2021' (2025) *Criminal Law Review* 750.

18 P Dargue, 'The Tolerability of Risk in the Court of Appeal (Criminal Division): An Empirical Study of Appeals against Conviction 2015–2021' (2025) *Criminal Law Review* 750.

19 P Dargue, 'The Tolerability of Risk in the Court of Appeal (Criminal Division): An Empirical Study of Appeals against Conviction 2015–2021' (2025) *Criminal Law Review* 752.

20 P Dargue, 'The Tolerability of Risk in the Court of Appeal (Criminal Division): An Empirical Study of Appeals against Conviction 2015–2021' (2025) *Criminal Law Review* 753–754. But note while procedural irregularities were the most *frequently* successful, they were *proportionally* less likely to be successful than fresh evidence.

21 P Dargue, 'The Tolerability of Risk in the Court of Appeal (Criminal Division): An Empirical Study of Appeals against Conviction 2015–2021' (2025) *Criminal Law Review* 751–752.

22 P Dargue, 'The Tolerability of Risk in the Court of Appeal (Criminal Division): An Empirical Study of Appeals against Conviction 2015–2021' (2025) *Criminal Law Review* 751.

of success of grounds of appeal; for instance allegations that the trial judge wrongly included / excluded evidence was successful only 8% of the times raised, while appeals concerning summing up irregularities were successful 17% of the times they were raised, and issues relating to jurisdiction were successful 100% of the time.[23] Appeals in which permission to adduce fresh evidence was given were successful 50% of the times it was raised.[24]

The unsafety test

Historical overview

The unsafety test is a product of its history, and so it is necessary to briefly detail some of this history.[25] The Court of Criminal Appeal (as the Court of Appeal (Criminal Division) was known until 1966) was created by the Criminal Appeal Act 1907. Section 4 provided that it shall allow and appeal if:

> The verdict of the jury should be set aside on the ground that it is *unreasonable or cannot be supported having regard to the evidence*, or there was *a wrong decision of any question of law* or *there was a miscarriage of justice*.
>
> (emphasis added)

As the 1907 Bill was passing through Parliament, FE Smith tabled an amendment to the 'unreasonable or not supported by the evidence' part of the aforementioned clause. He proposed that the Court should quash a conviction where it was 'unsafe or unsatisfactory'.[26] He thought it difficult to see how a court of review could consider a verdict of guilty to be unreasonable or not supported by the evidence if there was evidence available to convict.[27] He did not explain what he meant by the word 'unsafe'. He described it as having been used in the report to the *Edalji* case.[28] That report said that there are cases where new evidence 'without establishing the innocence of the prisoner, throws sufficient doubt on the conviction to make it unsafe'.[29] The report also said, 'we do not think it is at all safe to infer that [the letters] are the letters of a guilty man'.[30] It also did not explain what it meant by safety and unsafety.

23 P Dargue, 'The Tolerability of Risk in the Court of Appeal (Criminal Division): An Empirical Study of Appeals against Conviction 2015–2021' (2025) *Criminal Law Review* 753–754.

24 P Dargue, 'The Tolerability of Risk in the Court of Appeal (Criminal Division): An Empirical Study of Appeals against Conviction 2015–2021' (2025) *Criminal Law Review* 756.

25 For a much more detailed history see R Pattenden, *English Criminal Appeals 1844–1994* (Clarendon Press, 1996).

26 Parl Deb HC 29 July 1907, vol 179 col 633–636.

27 Hansard (n 26), vol 179 col 634.

28 Hansard (n 26), vol 179 col 635. The facts of which are immaterial for the purposes of the present discussion. See Home Office, *Papers Relating to the Case of George Edalji* (Cd. 3503, 1907).

29 *Edalji* (n 28) 8.

30 *Edalji* (n 28) 3.

Smith thought that the word 'unsafe' was perfectly intelligible, and unlike the 'unreasonable' wording, would provide the country with the appeal system it demanded: 'a really effective appeal on matters of fact where there had been a miscarriage of justice in the Court below'.[31]

The Attorney General, Sir John Walton, dismissed the amendment, saying that Smith could not have got the wording from a lawyer, and that the proposed tests were 'loose to the point of obscurity and unscientific, inasmuch as they would have no precision'.[32] He did not know what Smith or the *Edalji* report meant by 'unsafety', but thought that it must have some connection to the 'cannon of safety' relating to public safety.[33] Satisfied that his point had been made and understood, Smith withdrew his amendment. Sixty years later, Smith was vindicated when the Criminal Appeal Act 1966 enacted that wording.

The 1907 Act was in force for nearly 60 years before being amended by the Criminal Appeal Act 1966. The problem was the *unreasonable or cannot be supported having regard to the evidence* part of section 4. As early as 1911, Ross observed that appeals were rarely successful on that ground alone.[34] The Court's apparent approach was seen in a case such as *Allen*, in which the appeal was dismissed because it was 'quite impossible to say that the verdict was one which a jury might not reasonably find'.[35] Since the jury did find, this seems to set a high standard to have an appeal allowed. Throughout the Court's time applying the 1907 Act, there was reference to appellants seeking to have cases retried before the Court, with a rebuke that this was not the function of the Court.[36] In *Simpson* the Court said that the case was not a strong one, and it would have been open to the jury to acquit, but that the verdict must stand.[37]

Do these decisions show the Court taking an unduly narrow approach to its powers in section 4? It is submitted that a more charitable interpretation is that such pronouncements echo almost exactly what the Attorney General said the Court should do. He said of the proposed court that if a jury 'properly instructed could not have arrived at the conclusion at which the jury had arrived then they might set it aside, *but only then*'.[38] On this basis, it does not seem clear that the Court was not operating the test as enacted, or that its approach was open to serious criticism.[39] In any event, the Court would

31 Hansard (n 26), vol 179 col 635–636.
32 Hansard (n 26), vol 179 col 638.
33 Hansard (n 26), vol 179 col 638–639.
34 RE Ross, *The Court of Criminal Appeal* (Butterwort and Co., 1911) 88.
35 (1909) 1 Cr App R 18.
36 See *R v Lovett* (1909) 1 Cr App R 111; *R v Mason* (1909) 1 Cr App R 73; *R v Martin* (1909) 1 Cr App R 52.
37 (1909) 2 Cr App R 128.
38 Parl Deb HC 29 July 1907, vol 179 col 638–7 (emphasis added).
39 This was the conclusion of the Donovan Committee, Lord Chancellor's Office, Interdepartmental Committee on the Court of Criminal Appeal, *Report* (1965 Cmnd 2755) [141] (to be discussed further). It is submitted that the Committee was right in that conclusion.

often quash convictions owing to deficiencies with the evidence. For instance, in *Lee*[40] Lord Alverstone said that a miscarriage of justice had occurred and quashed the conviction. In *Laws*[41] the Court admitted fresh evidence of alibi and quashed the conviction. In *Osborne*[42] a conviction was quashed because the Court had 'very serious doubt as to the appellant's guilt'.[43] In 1951 Davies that the Court had displayed a 'sensibly liberal attitude' and was a 'a great bulwark against miscarriages of justice'.[44] It is important to keep in mind, therefore, that it is possible to disagree with the notion that the Court has consistently adopted a narrow approach.

In 1964 the organisation *Justice* issued a highly critical review of the Court, stating that it had taken a very restricted view of its powers.[45] The government had already convened the Donovan Committee to investigate its approach.[46] The Committee thought that the wording of section 4 constrained the Court's power to quash convictions because it required the conviction be 'unreasonable' or 'not supported by the evidence'. Since the jury convicted, there must have been evidence; otherwise it was an error of the trial judge for not stopping the case (i.e. it would fall under the 'wrong decision of any question of law' ground, not the 'unreasonable' ground). The Committee proposed amending the Court's powers to induce the Court to act in a way that 'so far as possible' any miscarriages of justice will be avoided or corrected.[47]

The Donovan Committee's proposals were enacted by the Criminal Appeal Act 1966, which was subsequently consolidated by the Criminal Appeal Act 1968. In line with the Committee's recommendations, section 2 of the 1968 Act read that the Court was to allow an appeal if it thought the conviction was:

(a) unsafe or unsatisfactory, or
(b) there was a wrong decision on a question of law, or
(c) there had been a material irregularity.

It can be seen that, in effect, the 'unsafe or unsatisfactory' element of the 1968 Act replaced the '*unreasonable or cannot be supported having regard to the evidence*' element of the 1907 Act.

The Court operated this test until the enactment of the Criminal Appeal Act 1995. The reason for its reform was the report of the *Royal Commission*

40 (1909) 1 Cr App R 5.
41 (1909) 1 Cr App R 6.
42 (1909) 1 Cr App R 144.
43 *Osborne* (n 42).
44 D Seabourne Davies, 'The Court of Criminal Appeal: The First Forty Years' (1951) 1 *Journal of the Society of Public Teachers of Law* (N.S) 425, 431.
45 Justice, *Criminal Appeals* (Stevens and Sons, 1964) 59.
46 Donovan Committee (n 39).
47 Donovan Committee (n 39) 136.

on Criminal Justice (RCCJ).[48] The RCCJ was convened in 1991 and reported in 1993. It was convened following the quashing of the convictions of the *Birmingham Six*, which is regarded as one of the most significant miscarriages of justice in the criminal history of England and Wales.[49] The performance of the Court of Appeal, the RCCJ noted, 'is crucial to the early correction of miscarriages of justice' however they are generated, including where the jury has come to 'the wrong verdict on the evidence it did hear'.[50] Research conducted on behalf of the RCCJ, by Malleson, found that often the Court spoke in terms of whether the conviction is 'unsafe or unsatisfactory' rather than any of the other two grounds, even when one of the other grounds seemed more appropriate.[51] The RCCJ thought that the Court's approach had 'been too heavily influenced by the role of the jury in Crown Court trials', and it should 'be readier to overturn jury verdicts than it had shown itself to be in the past'.[52] It thus recommended adoption of the unsafety test, as well as the creation of the CCRC.

With the enactment of the 1995 Act, all of grounds (b) and (c) and half of (a) to section 2 of the 1968 Act were deleted. The deletion, in particular, of (b) and (c) may lead to the impression that it was intended that convictions could no longer be quashed on those bases. However, in Parliament, the unsafety test was said to restate the existing practice of the Court.[53] This was apparently the view of the Lord Chief Justice (Lord Taylor) and the senior judiciary at the time.[54] But, as noted earlier, the key intention behind the recommendation of the unsafety test by the RCCJ was not that it should be narrower, nor that it should be a restatement, but that it should induce a more liberal approach. Smith's analysis of the unsafety test shortly after its enactment is particularly pertinent now, given the reasonable foreseeability of legislative reform in the future. He said that since the 'unsafe or unsatisfactory' element of the 1968 Act amounted to no more or less than the question of whether the appellant was wrongly convicted, and it was that element of the 1968 Act which survived the 1995 amendment, the amendment to the single 'unsafety' test could have no substantive effect and the Court would continue to reach the same decisions as it had in the past.[55]

48 Royal Commission on Criminal Justice, *Report* (Cm 2263, 1993).

49 See *R v McIlkenny and others* (1991) 93 Cr App R 28. See also C Mullin, *Error of Judgment: The Truth about the Birmingham Bombings* (Poolbeg Press, 1990).

50 RCCJ (n 48) 162.

51 K Malleson, *The Royal Commission on Criminal Justice Research Study No 17* (HMSO, 1993).

52 RCCJ (n 48) 162.

53 See discussion by the Law Commission, *Criminal Appeals: Consultation Paper* (Law Comm No 268, 2025) [8.26].

54 Law Commission (n 53) [8.26]. See also J Smith, 'The Criminal Appeal Act 1995: Part 1: Appeals against Conviction' (1995) *Criminal Law Review* 920.

55 Smith (n 54) 924–925.

The meaning of unsafety

The word 'unsafe' was not entirely unknown to the criminal law prior to its enactment in the Criminal Appeal Act 1968.[56] As the Court explained in *Lewis,* in the law relating to corroboration, it was the law that the trial judge was to 'warn the jury that it is unsafe to convict on the uncorroborated evidence of an accomplice'.[57] That would seem to have come from Stephen's *Digest.*[58] Prior to the 1968 Act, appeals would occasionally appear before the Court in which the appellant complained that this direction was not given, and the Court would frequently quash the conviction if it found the direction was not given.[59] The earlier pages of the *Criminal Appeal Reports* show occasional reference by judges or counsel to the concept of safety rather than the terms of the 1907 Act.[60] The primary rationale provided in the Donovan Committee for the adoption of 'unsafe or unsatisfactory' as the test was a) FE Smith had proposed it earlier, and b) the Court would sometimes refer to 'unsafety' in any event.[61]

Thus, how it was that the word 'unsafe' came to signify that a conviction must be quashed is rather vague, but is oddly appropriate. The concept of safety / unsafety has developed its own discrete meaning in the context of criminal appeals without, it would seem, any significant recourse to the broader general concepts of risk and safety. This is unfortunate, because there is much that can be gleaned from the general concept of risk (see Chapter 2). The unsafety test as enacted by the Criminal Appeal Act 1995 does not provide any direction, or any floor or ceiling to its exercise. It is to some extent blowing around in the wind. The Act quite simply says that the Court shall allow an appeal 'if they think' the conviction is unsafe.

One might consider it a word that attempts to 'thingify' the rather inchoate and nebulous feeling that courts should quash convictions when an injustice would be done were it left to stand. After all, doing justice is the Court's role. As per Cohen's classic discussion of the idea of thingification, just as nobody has ever seen 'a corporation', nobody has ever seen an 'unsafe conviction'.[62] A conviction only becomes unsafe (or, indeed, safe) once it enters the doors of Royal Courts of Justice and the Court gifts it with that label. Ultimately, the unsafety test requires the Court to allow and dismiss whatever appeals

56 As discussed earlier, it was used by JE Smith and in the *Edalji* case.

57 *R v Lewis* (1938) 26 Cr App R 110,113.

58 J Stephen, *A Digest on the Law of Evidence* (5th edn, 1887) art. 121. See *R v Baskerville* [1916] 2 KB 658.

59 Eg *R v Baskerville* [1916] 2 KB 658; *R v Phillips* (1925) 18 Cr App R 115; *R v Parker* (1925) 18 Cr App R 103; *R v Mason* (1910) 5 Cr App R 171.

60 Eg. *R v Treloar* (1914) 9 Cr App R 1; *R v Baxter* (1914) 9 Cr App R 60; *R v Franks* (1916) 11 Cr App R 104.

61 See Donovan (n 39) 144–149.

62 See F E Cohen, 'Transcendental Nonsense and the Functional Approach' (1935) 35 (6) *Columbia Law Review* 809, 811.

it thinks ought to be allowed and dismissed in order to do justice, and that decision is then given legal effect. As Nobles and Schiff said, one should not take statutory powers such as the unsafety test too literally because the judges of the Court will 'draw on their experience as advocates and judges in deciding what procedures are significant'.[63] Whilst this is true, it is submitted that the Court will generally do what it is told to do, and it is currently told to simply consider whether the conviction is unsafe.

The inchoate nature of the test does have a knock-on effect. Each case before the Court is unique and fact-specific. Appeals are decided on their particular circumstances. There is hardly any necessary connection between any two cases; the same kind of error does not mean the same outcome will prevail. Thus, when the Court says in case *X* that it thinks the conviction is safe and so it will not reverse the verdict of the jury, there is nothing to stop it in case *Y* doing precisely that. Since the question for the Court is whether *they think* the conviction is unsafe, and the Court will draw upon its experience to decide whether they think it is unsafe, it is impossible for that decision to be either right or wrong. This is why Pattenden was able to describe the Court as being like 'broken compass which swings erratically between North and South' and as being 'confused and inconsistent about the values it promotes'.[64] Swinging North might be what the Court thinks is required by justice in case *X*, while swinging South is what is required in case *Y*.

Allowing or dismissing an appeal is essentially in the gift of the judges who are hearing a particular appeal on a particular day; it is discretionary. Given that any number of things can go wrong during the course of the criminal process, it would be impossible for any Act of Parliament to set out all the circumstances that could lead to an appeal being unsafe. It might be said that the test falls into Hart's 'penumbra' where the law has run out and decisions rely on the exercise of discretion.[65] It is possible to imagine that over time (perhaps in a few hundred years) the penumbra might be filled and every possible factual scenario has a judgment from the Court on the 'definition' of unsafety. Until such time, however, the unsafety test itself does not provide any guideline, or guard rails, as to what degree of protection the Court should be providing, and what the balance should be between freeing the innocent and convicting the guilty. It will be explained in more detail in Chapter 2 how recourse to the concept of risk can assist in this regard. Before doing so, it is important to understand how the courts have interpreted the word in the context of criminal appeals.

Particularly important regarding the general meaning of the term 'unsafety' in the context of criminal appeals is *Cooper*, decided shortly after the enactment

63 R Nobles, D Schiff, *Understanding Miscarriages of Justice: The Law, The Media, and the Inevitability of Crisis* (Oxford University Press, 2000) 88–89.

64 Pattenden (n 25) 210.

65 H L A Hart, *The Concept of Law* (3rd edn, Oxford University Press, 2012) 129–131.

of the 1968 Act.[66] All the relevant material had been before the jury, and there was no criticism of the summing up. The appellant could not point to anything new that had not been before the jury; he submitted that the jury had got it wrong due to misidentification of him as the attacker. Lord Widgery said that under the 'unsafe or unsatisfactory test', the Court must:[67]

> Ask itself a subjective question, whether we are content to let the matter stand as it is, or whether there is not some lurking doubt in our minds which makes us wonder whether an injustice has been done. This is a reaction which may not be based strictly on the evidence as such; it is a reaction which can be produced by the general feel of the case as the Court experiences it.

The conviction was quashed. This judgment has given rise to the term 'lurking doubt' in the context of criminal appeals. This could be considered a significant turning-point in the jurisprudence of the Court, because, as Lord Widgery observed, it had been said 'over and over throughout the years that this Court must recognise the advantage which a jury has . . . and should not lightly interfere'.[68] Knight's study of the Court observed a change in approach after this decision.[69] *Cooper* would potentially mean that the Court would be more open to quashing convictions where there was no irregularity or fresh evidence, and the Court had a subjective sense of unease.

The most detailed explanation of the general meaning of the unsafety test under the 1995 Act was in the case of *Pearson.*[70] Lord Bingham said that some examples of unsafety will be obvious, such as:[71]

> Where it appears that someone other than the appellant committed the crime and the appellant did not, or where the appellant has been convicted of an act that was not in law a crime, or where a conviction is shown to be vitiated by serious unfairness in the conduct of the trial or significant legal misdirection, or where the jury verdict, in the context of other verdicts, defies any rational explanation.

In these circumstances, the conviction will be unsafe. There will be other less obvious cases in which the Court:[72]

> Although by no means persuaded of an appellant's innocence, is subject to some lurking doubt or uneasiness whether an injustice has been done . . . If,

66 (1969) 53 Cr App R 82.
67 *Cooper* (n 66) 86.
68 *Cooper* (n 66) 85.
69 M Knight, *Criminal Appeals* (Stevens and Sons, 1970) 135. See also M Knight, *Criminal Appeals Supplement 1969–1973* (Stevens and Sons, 1975).
70 [2000] 1 Cr App R 141.
71 *Pearson* (n 70) 146.
72 *Pearson* (n 70) 146–147.

> on consideration of all the facts and circumstances of the case before it, the Court entertains real doubts whether the appellant was guilty of the offence of which he has been convicted, the Court will consider the conviction unsafe. In these less obvious cases the ultimate decision of the Court of Appeal will very much depend on its assessment of all the facts and circumstances.

It ought to be noted that the unsafety test does not require that the appellant proves his innocence. As Mantell LJ said in *Davis, Rowe, and Johnson*:[73]

> The Court is concerned with the safety of the conviction. A conviction can never be safe if there is doubt about guilt. However, the converse is not true. A conviction may be unsafe even where there is no doubt about guilt but the trial process has been vitiated by serious unfairness or significant legal misdirection.

The unsafety test is broadly protective of appellants' due process and fair trial rights. If the trial process has been 'vitiated' by irregularity it must be quashed even if the appellant cannot directly challenge the facts underling his conviction.[74] With this general understanding of the meaning of unsafety, the Court's decision-making approach in the three kinds of appeals that appear before it (lurking doubt, procedural irregularity, fresh evidence) can now be explained. It is convenient to start with the concept of lurking doubt.

Lurking doubt

The concept of doubt is subsumed within the unsafety test and forms part of it. The examples of 'obvious' unsafety referred to in *Pearson* might be considered part of the upper boundary of unsafety: things that an appellant can directly point to that will, if the Court agrees, cause the conviction to cross the threshold into unsafety. A lurking doubt, meanwhile, is the lower boundary of unsafety, a more inchoate feeling about a case. Nevertheless, if the conviction crosses that boundary it must be unsafe. To a very real extent, therefore, lurking doubt is the essence of the unsafety test; if a conviction crosses this lower boundary due to the Court having (at least) a lurking doubt, everything else is superfluous and the conviction is unsafe. It follows that all allowed appeals must have (at least) a lurking doubt that an injustice was done, and all dismissed appeals there could not have been such a doubt.

The Court of Appeal has since retreated from the position in *Cooper*. In *Pope* Lord Judge said that the Court cannot quash a conviction on the basis of 'subjective judicial hunch'; there should instead be 'reasoned analysis of the evidence or the trial process, or both, which leads to the inexorable conclusion

73 [2001] 1 Cr App R 8, 132.

74 See for example *R v Mullen* (1999) 2 Cr App R 143.

that the conviction is unsafe'.[75] The Court has consistently depreciated use of the phrase 'lurking doubt' or sought to suggest it is not a valid ground of appeal.[76] As Taylor and Fitzgerald told the Law Commission, the Court's hostility towards the phrase 'lurking doubt' is difficult to reconcile with the unsafety test given the unsafety test requires it to decide whether *they think* (i.e. a subjective feeling) the conviction is unsafe.[77]

It is suggested that the real reason for the Court's hostility towards the phrase 'lurking doubt' is the rather murky phrase itself. If it was genuinely hostile to quashing convictions when the Court has a doubt, this is contrary to the wording of the unsafety test. As shown in Chapter 3 of this book, the Court does quash convictions with some regularity not only for 'obvious' types of unsafety, but the less obvious kinds based on a feeling of unease. It is important to note that Lord Widgery's use of the phrase 'lurking doubt' in *Cooper* was unprecedented,[78] and could be regarded as a form of words chosen by a particular judge on a particular day to explain his particular understanding of the unsafe or unsatisfactory test. To that extent, perhaps it should not be taken too literally. The word 'lurking' is suggestive of some hidden, nefarious doubt and brings to mind a doubt which is 'lurking in the shadows'. But the Court cannot quash convictions on the basis of hidden doubts – as Lord Judge said in *Pope* the doubt must come to the foreground through the reasoned assessment of the evidence.

Procedural irregularity

Where procedural irregularity is raised as a ground of appeal, the first stage is for the Court to determine whether the irregularity occurred. The Court will make use of the transcript of the summing up and the transcript of any *voir dire* in which an evidential decision was made. The Court will typically make up its mind as to what was a correct statement of the law / correct use of discretion by using precedential cases before determining whether the trial judge in the instant case made a correct decision.

In *Hanson*,[79] a key case on the topic of the admissibility of bad character, the Court of Appeal said that it would only intervene with a trial judge's exercise of a judgment, so long as he has not misdirected himself, if it is 'plainly wrong', or a discretion if it has if it was exercised unreasonably in

75 *R v Pope* [2012] EWCA Crim 2241 [14].

76 Eg *R v D* [2013] EWCA Crim 1592. It might be for this reason that lurking doubt does not appear very often as a ground of appeal.

77 Law Commission (n 48) [8.115].

78 A search of *Westlaw* showed no use of that phrase in the context of criminal appeals before *Cooper*.

79 *R v Hanson and others* [2005] EWCA Crim 824.

the *Wednesbury* sense.[80] *Wednesbury* unreasonableness requires a decision or conduct that is so unreasonable no judge could have reasonably came to it.[81] This approach has been repeated many times.[82] In *W* the Court said that the Court can only intervene in the Court's power of exclusionary discretion under section 78 of the Police and Criminal Evidence Act 1984 if the trial judge's exercise of their discretion was *Wednesbury* unreasonable.[83] This is a difficult hurdle for an appellant to surmount and provides considerable latitude to the trial judge. The reason for this deference was recently explained in *Al-Shumari* as being due because 'the assessment made by a trial judge is highly fact-sensitive and his or her feel for the case is often crucial'.[84]

Where the Court finds that no irregularity occurred, and there is no fresh evidence, the Court remains compelled to determine whether the conviction is safe. (As per Mantell LJ in *Davis* (mentioned previously), a conviction can never be safe where there is doubt about guilt). In effect these 'no error' cases are converted into 'lurking doubt' appeals even if the appellant does not use that phrase himself. The Court is required, in *Pope* terms, to conduct a reasoned analysis of the evidence in order to assess whether it reaches the inexorable conclusion that the conviction is unsafe. If it is not doing this then it is not exercising the unsafety test as articulated in *Pearson, Davis*, and / or *Cooper*.

In an earlier study of the Court, it was found that most appellants (63%) were unable to convince the Court that any irregularity occurred in the process at all.[85] In a sample of 931 cases, that represented 586 cases: approximately 100 per year. Whilst appeals directly using the phrase 'lurking doubt' were virtually non-existent in this earlier study,[86] they accordingly form a large bulk of the Court's workload where the Court finds that no irregularity occurred in the earlier parts of the criminal process. The earlier study found that these kinds of appeal would be inevitably dismissed unless the appellant also had fresh evidence.[87]

In *Davis* (mentioned earlier), the Court said that when an irregularity does arise, it is to ask whether, had the irregularity had not occurred, 'would the only reasonable and proper verdict have been one of guilty?'[88] If the only reasonable and proper verdict would have been one of guilty, the conviction will be safe; otherwise it must be quashed. The Court is required to embark upon an

80 *Hanson* (n 79) 15.
81 *Associated Provincial Pictures Houses Ltd v Wednesbury Corp* [1948] 1 KB 223.
82 Eg in *R v Byrne* [2021] EWCA Crim 107; *R v Rowe* [2022] EWCA Crim 27; *R v Khan* [2022] EWCA Crim 1010.
83 [2022] EWCA Crim 1438, [42].
84 [2025] EWCA Crim 1317, [74].
85 Dargue (n 16) 753.
86 Dargue (n 16) 752.
87 Dargue (n 16) 753.
88 *Davis* (n 73) 132.

exercise of counterfactual reasoning by determining the link between the error and the logic required of the jury to convict. In general, where the irregularity goes directly to that logic the conviction must be quashed; otherwise it can be upheld. In Dargue's earlier study, if the Court found that the alleged error did occur, which happened in 37% of cases, 66% of those were allowed.[89] Thus, an appellant who can adduce and convince the Court that an irregularity occurred in the process has a good chance of having their conviction quashed.

Fresh evidence

There are two separate issues for the Court to address in fresh evidence cases: first, whether the fresh evidence should be admitted, and second, whether the evidence renders the conviction unsafe. In relation to the first question, the test for admission is the interests of justice, with the subsection (2) factors (provided previously) to assist in that question. *Erskine*[90] affirmed the Court's general view that the factors (a) – (d) are neither exhaustive nor conclusive, but require specific attention.[91]

The next question is how the Court should determine whether the fresh evidence (once admitted) renders the conviction unsafe. In *Stafford and Luvaglio*[92] Viscount Dilhorne said that the Court's approach in fresh evidence is not a question of law: 'the Act does not require the court, in making up its mind whether or not a verdict is unsafe or unsatisfactory, to apply any particular test'.[93] He confirmed that the question in fresh evidence appeals is whether the Court itself has a doubt about safety, a subjective test. It is not sufficient that the fresh evidence is thought credible and admissible, or could have impacted the jury (what is known as the 'jury impact' test); it must actually cause the Court some doubt about safety. On this, he said:

> Parliament has not required or given [the Court the] power to quash a verdict if they think that a jury might conceivably reach a different conclusion from that to which they have come. If the court has no reasonable doubt about the verdict, it follows that the court does not think that the jury could have one; and, conversely, if the court says that a jury might in the light of the new evidence have a reasonable doubt, that means that the court has a reasonable doubt.[94]

Stafford remains good law today, but has been somewhat superseded by *Pendleton*.[95] In that case Lord Bingham said that 'save in a clear case' the

89 Dargue (n 16) 753.
90 [2009] EWCA Crim 1425.
91 *Erskine* (n 90) 39.
92 [1974] AC 878.
93 *Stafford* (n 92) 891.
94 *Stafford* (n 92) 893.
95 [2001] UKHL 66.

Court is at a disadvantage compared to the jury in seeking to relate the fresh evidence to all the evidence the jury heard.[96] As such:

> It will usually be wise for the Court of Appeal, in a case of any difficulty, to test their own provisional view by asking whether the evidence, if given at trial, might reasonably have affected the decision of the jury to convict. If it might, the conviction must be thought unsafe.[97]

This appears to mean that it will usually be wise for the Court to apply the 'jury impact' test, and assess whether, if a jury had seen the evidence, it could reasonably have affected the decision of the jury to convict.

A court under scrutiny

The preceding pages might give the impression that all is calm and settled in the Court of Appeal. But this is not the case. There is a common view amongst some academics, practitioners, prisoners, and campaigners that the Court is in some general sense unduly cautious in choosing which appeals to allow and which to dismiss. The Court has been referred to as being in 'dereliction of duty' for this approach,[98] and a 'significant obstacle to addressing miscarriages of justice'.[99] Justice, according to Naughton, was 'aborted from day one . . . by judges who collectively refused to overturn convictions on facts that had already been decided at the trial of first instance'.[100] Roberts concluded that the Court is 'deficient at rectifying the wrongful convictions of the factually innocent' due to a narrow approach towards fresh evidence.[101]

The key claims are that the Court generally shows too much deference to the jury, it has too much reverence to the principle of finality, and it is motivated by fear of opening the floodgates to a deluge of appeals.[102] This view has been supported by empirical research and the Court's statistics following the enactment of the unsafety test, the Court's general statements throughout its history as to the primacy of the jury, and the Court's decision-making in individual cases. The fact that the Court's powers had to be re-written in the

96 *Pendleton* (n 95) 19.

97 *Pendleton* (n 95) 19.

98 See Supplementary written evidence from Professor Michael Zander QC to the Justice Committee 12th Report of Session 2014–15, *Criminal Cases Review Commission* (2015 HC 850).

99 See House of Commons Justice Committee, Criminal Cases Review Commission Twelfth Report of Session 2014–5 (2015 HV 850) 14, citing Stephen Heaton.

100 M Naughton, *The Innocent and the Criminal Justice System: A Sociological Analysis of Miscarriages of Justice* (Palgrave MacMillan, 2013) 160.

101 S Roberts, 'Fresh Evidence and Factual Innocence in the Criminal Division of the Court of Appeal' (2017) 81 (4) *Criminal Law Review* 304, 304.

102 See C McCartney, S Roberts, 'Building Institutions to Address Miscarriages of Justice in England and Wales: "Mission Accomplished?"' (2013) 80 (4) *University of Cincinnati Law Review* 1333, 1337.

1960s and in 1995, principally due to concerns around the Court's approach, can act as evidence of the Court's narrow approach.

As to statistics, in simple quantitative terms it is not easy to have an appeal allowed. Empirical research by, for instance, Malleson[103] and Roberts,[104] has shown the Court's apparent resistance to quashing convictions on the basis of a lurking doubt, deference towards the jury and finality, and apparent resistance to admitting fresh evidence. Dargue's research showed that fresh evidence was comparatively rare, and that it is virtually impossible to have an appeal allowed if there is no fresh evidence or procedural irregularity.[105] Throughout its history the Court has consistently stated that the jury is in a better position than it to determine facts, and that the Court will not re-try appellants with a view to reversing jury verdicts. It is also the case that, throughout its history and repeatedly, the Court has made numerous 'mistakes' by dismissing appeals from appellants that now appear to be innocent. Well-recognised miscarriages of justice, such as the *Birmingham Six* (previously mentioned), *Stefan Kiszko*,[106] and *Andrew Malkinson*,[107] all had appeals dismissed, some repeatedly.

In light of these concerns about the Court's approach, the 2015 House of Commons Justice Committee recommended that the appeal system be reviewed by the Law Commission.[108] That view was repeated by the All-Party Parliamentary Group on Miscarriages of Justice in 2021.[109] Both the 2015 and 2021 reports had the CCRC as their primary focus, but heard evidence that the approach of the Court of Appeal was problematic.[110] Even a former Court of Appeal judge, cited in the 2021 report, thought that it had become much more difficult for an appellant to succeed than what it had been.[111] According to the 2021 report, the evidence it had heard 'suggests that the Court of Appeal's approach to cases may prevent some miscarriages of justice being corrected'.[112] This echoed what the

103 Malleson (n 51).

104 Roberts (n 101).

105 Dargue (n 16).

106 Mr Kiszko was convicted of the 1975 murder of Lesley Molseed. In 1999 it became apparent that DNA left at the scene could not have come from him. His conviction was quashed after 16 years of imprisonment. Another man has since been convicted; see *R v Castree* [2008] EWCA Crim 1866. Kiszko had applied for permission to appeal in 1978, but was denied permission, see *R v Kiszko* (1979) 68 Cr App R 62, a serious blunder by the Court.

107 See *R v Malkinson* [2023] EWCA Crim 954, where his convictions were quashed. He had also appealed unsuccessfully in 2006 [2006] EWCA Crim 1891, leading to an additional 16 years of wrongful imprisonment.

108 Justice Committee (n 99).

109 All Party Parliamentary Group on Miscarriages of Justice, *In the Interests of Justice: An Inquiry into the Criminal Cases Review Commission* (HMSO, 2021).

110 See the 2015 report (n 99) 13, 2021 report (n 109) 40.

111 2021 report (n 109) 40.

112 2021 report (n 109) 21.

Committee said in 2015: that the central complaint against the Court is that it is 'overly reluctant to interfere with a properly delivered jury verdict'.[113]

In its consultation paper, the Law Commission said that the Court 'sometimes takes too narrow a view' of whether fresh evidence or identification of legal error renders a conviction unsafe.[114] It also observed that, in practice, the Court is highly unlikely to quash a conviction if a properly directed jury has convicted on the evidence, and there is no fresh evidence or procedural irregularity.[115] In relation to fresh evidence, the Commission said there was force in the criticism that it interpreted its powers narrowly, in that there was a 'presumption of unreliability and inadmissibility' towards certain kinds of fresh evidence.[116] It ultimately proposed that where the Court admits fresh evidence, believing it to be relevant and capable of belief, that could have led the jury to acquit, the Court should quash the conviction and order a retrial if possible.[117] This would take the question of whether the evidence renders the conviction unsafe out of the Court's hands, remedying the allegedly unduly cautious approach towards fresh evidence.[118]

Some criticism of some criticisms

The Court has consistently stated that it will not quash convictions, in the absence of any irregularity or fresh evidence, merely on the basis that the jury could have acquitted. An appellant, who may be innocent, will accordingly find it difficult to succeed unless he can happen to locate a legal error or fresh evidence. The Court could if it wanted to, and is often asked to, re-appraise the evidence and consider whether the jury should have convicted, rather than only consider whether the process was properly followed and whether there was sufficient evidence to convict. It could be more open to quashing convictions, despite the jury deciding to convict, where the evidence is finely balanced. This invitation is one that the Court has strongly resisted.

The key reason for this resistance is that reconsidering the jury's verdict would be to 'usurp' the role of the jury.[119] Lord Bingham summarised its reluctance to do so in *Pendleton*:[120]

> [Counsel] is right to emphasise the central role of the jury in a trial on indictment. This is an important and greatly-prized feature of our constitution.

113 2021 report (n 109) 13.
114 Law Commission (n 53) [8.123].
115 Law Commission (n 53) [8.144].
116 Law Commission (n 53) [6.73].
117 Law Commission (n 53) [8.126–127].
118 This reform is considered in more detail in Chapter 4 of this book.
119 See S Roberts, 'Reviewing the Function of the Criminal Appeals in England and Wales' (2017) 1 *Institute of Law Journal* 1, 20.
120 *Pendleton* (n 95) 17. (Emphasis added).

> Trial by jury does not mean trial by jury in the first instance and trial by judges of the Court of Appeal in the second. The Court of Appeal is entrusted with a power of review to guard against the possibility of injustice *but it is a power to be exercised with caution*, mindful that the Court of Appeal is not privy to the jury's deliberations and must not intrude into territory which properly belongs to the jury.

Lord Bingham, therefore, accepted that the Court's approach is 'cautious' and that it will not stray into the territory of the jury. The literature on criminal appeals tends to refer to the Court having generally adopted a narrow, reluctant, or restrictive approach. It is not clear whether there is any real difference between the word 'cautious' and these alternative words. Clearly, the way those words are used by critics is more pejorative than the word 'cautious' and indicates that the particular approach is not desirable. But both 'cautious' and for instance 'narrow' indicate that it is not easy to have an appeal allowed, and that much, as noted, is a fact. The allegation of a generally narrow etc approach is not, therefore, an objective statement of fact; it is an interpretation / assessment of the Court's statistics, words, and outcomes.

It is not obvious that the usual words used in the criticism of the Court's approach necessarily always carry negative connotations. While 'narrow minded' probably is always understood negatively, 'narrow focussed' might not be; it depends upon the particular interpretation given to the words. Furthermore, one may rightly be 'reluctant' to do something one does not want to do or what one thinks is against one's better judgement. One may think there are good reasons to 'restrict' the movement or freedom of convicted murderers, for instance. Whether one views the Court as being narrow or not is subjective, and largely dependent upon how seriously one wants to confront the problem of miscarriages of justice *vis* the need to also convict perpetrators. In that regard, it is important to remember that the judges of the Court take an oath of impartiality. They are directed both by that oath and the terms of the unsafety test not to have a pre-determined preference for either allowing or dismissing appeals; they are required to do what they think justice requires.

If 'cautious' means nearly the same as 'narrow', then there is no dispute between the critics and the Court. The Court accepts that it is cautious, and this is undeniable from the statistics demonstrating the difficulty in having a conviction quashed. But there is a dispute. The critics' words are usually modified by a word such as 'unduly' or 'overly', while the Court would not refer to itself as being 'overly' cautious. 'Overly' suggests that it is more cautious, or narrow, or reluctant, than what it should be, or perhaps it is more cautious than what it says it is. The real question, therefore, is whether its general approach, rather than being merely cautious, is overly cautious / narrow / restrictive, etc. If it is, this might be thought to constitute a rather light-touch level of judicial oversight that might 'expose the accused to inflated risks of wrongful conviction'.[121] Since the Court uses the word 'cautious' in describing its approach, that is the preferred word hereafter.

It is argued that since reform has happened in the past and there has been no observable change to the Court's allegedly unduly cautious approach, it is time to question the supposition that criticising the Court's alleged general approach in terms of its 'narrowness' is helpful or, indeed, accurate. The idea of a generally unduly cautious approach is too slippery to be helpful and should be abandoned. The unsafety test does not compel any particular approach; it does not tell the Court to be liberal or narrow, it tells the Court to do what it thinks is best. This is not to suggest that the Court does not make mistakes, nor is it to suggest that it can never be said the Court was wrong or unduly cautious at the micro level of a particular case. Reasonable people can disagree as to the outcome of appeals against conviction, and the Court can be legitimately criticised for being too narrow or using flawed reasoning in individual cases. However, it is argued that it is not possible to say that the Court is generally unduly cautious in relation to the test it has been provided, in terms of it having a settled 'approach' to be unduly cautious.

Although somewhat of a consensus that the Court's allegedly unduly cautious approach does exist, there are serious methodological problems associated with that assertion.[122] As Nobles and Schiff observed, Parliament delegated to the Court the power / duty to decide whether a conviction should be quashed – the unsafety test explicitly states that the conviction should be quashed 'if *they* think' the conviction is unsafe.[123] Since that is what the Court does, unless it is thought that the Court is operating some different test, how can it then be said that the Court is not performing its duties in the way envisioned by Parliament? Moreover, who determines whether the Court is not performing in line with its duties? Is it only the interests of appellants that are considered? As noted previously, a good criminal appeal system does justice to both the appellant and the prosecution. What of the (alleged) victims and complainants of the crimes of which the appellants were convicted? What of the public who want to see crimes prosecuted and perpetrators convicted? It is hard to imagine that they would subscribe to the view that the Court is generally unduly cautious.

121 P Roberts, A Zuckerman, *Roberts and Zuckerman's Criminal Evidence* (3rd edn, Oxford University Press, 2022) 99.

122 See R Nobles, D Schiff, 'The Never Ending Story: Disguising Tragic Choices in Criminal Justice' (1997) 60 (2) *Modern Law Review* 293, 294.

123 Nobles and Schiff (n 122) 294.

A further problem is envisioned by Roberts:[124]

> Whilst the consensus appears to suggest the Court is too reluctant to quash convictions, it is difficult to measure in any meaningful way whether the Court should be quashing more convictions . . . Whilst the consensus may suggest that the Court's approach to finality and deference leads it to be restrictive, the literature does not provide a gauge by which this should be measured.

The concession that it is difficult to measure whether the Court should be quashing more convictions seems fatal to the supposition of a generally unduly cautious approach. If it cannot be said that the Court should be quashing more convictions, then what does the allegation of an unduly cautious approach mean? As noted earlier, the Court accepts that it is cautious but it would be unlikely to accept that it is unduly cautious. In written evidence to the 2015 Justice Committee inquiry into the CCRC (cited previously) Lord Judge, the former Lord Chief Justice, said the following, with which he said the Lord Chief Justice at the time (Lord Thomas) agreed:[125]

> It is inevitable that from time to time the CACD will say something to the effect that the issues of credibility were considered by the jury and that there is no basis for interfering with their decision . . . Nevertheless, if having examined the evidence, the court is left in doubt about the safety of the conviction it must and will be quashed. The CACD cannot and does not approach its responsibilities by saying "we think the conviction may be unsafe but it will not be quashed because that would constitute an interference with the verdict or constitutional primacy of the jury".

If this is accurate, it seems to amount to a complete defence to the allegation of an unduly cautious approach. The first sentence of this passage summarises what is often said to characterise the Court's allegedly unduly cautious approach. Assuming that this letter is a genuine attempt by Lord Judge to describe decision-making in the Court, it appears that he is accusing its critics of taking the Court's words too literally. There is more than an element of truth to that allegation. The Court may slip into talk of refusing to interfere with the jury's verdict, but that does not mean they have not properly considered the evidence and that it is not prepared to reverse jury verdicts when it has doubts about it. The examination of the Court's routine decision-making presented in Chapter 3 of this book supports the supposition that the Court does properly assess the weight of the evidence, and it is difficult to see how such an approach would be considered unduly cautious.

124 Roberts (n 119) 5.
125 See https://committees.parliament.uk/writtenevidence/56689/pdf/.

It is also important to observe the obvious, but often overlooked, fact that the Court *does* quash convictions. The Court quashes several dozen convictions each year and has quashed many thousands over the course of its 120-year history. When the main focus is on the Court's allegedly unduly cautious approach, focusing primarily on unsuccessful appeals would tend to skew the analysis in that direction because the Court could hardly be considered overly cautious when it allows an appeal. Little is ever said of appellants who were successful, many of whom do not prove their innocence, and whether they would find the Court unduly cautious.

The Court could, if it so wished, allow all appeals if it decided that from now on all convictions are unsafe. There is nothing in the unsafety test to prevent that (although it is likely the Supreme Court or Parliament would have something to say about it). In practice, however, some appeals are allowed and some are dismissed. If it is difficult to know whether the Court should be quashing more convictions, it is equally difficult to know which appeals, amongst those that are dismissed in a given time period, were dismissed due to an unduly cautious approach. This is a serious methodological problem.[126] Unless it is known – without the benefit of hindsight – what the 'correct' answer to the appeal was, how can it be said that a decision was unduly cautious? The supposition of undue caution is a subjective assessment that overreaches its epistemological limits of empirical findings.[127] It is argued that this is also fatal to the supposition of an unduly cautious approach. If it is not possible to clearly demark when a decision of the Court to dismiss an appeal slips from being 'cautious-but-acceptable' to 'unduly cautious' then the allegation of a restrictive approach loses all its content and becomes meaningless.

The Court could be more generous and allow more appeals on the basis of fresh evidence or lurking doubt, but, as Roberts said previously, there is no gauge as to how generous the Court should be and when it should stop. Furthermore, it would be unreasonable to expect that the Court exercises its function with perfection, never making a mistake. As discussed in Chapter 2, perfection is not required anywhere else in any other sphere of life. Either the Court has cause to doubt the safety of the conviction or it does not, it is unclear how the Court could be extolled to be more liberal. As Quirk also observed, increasing the focus on lurking doubt and possible innocence would put appellants (either innocent or guilty) who were subject to unfairness or failure of procedure at increased risk.[128]

126 This point has been made before, see P Dargue, 'The Safety of Convictions in the Court of Appeal: Fresh Evidence in the Criminal Division through an Empirical Lens' (2019) 83 (6) *Journal of Criminal Law* 433. But it does not seem to have any appreciable impact on the assessment of the Court's apparent approach.

127 See also Dargue 2019 (n 126).

128 H Quirk, 'Identifying Miscarriages of Justice: Why Innocence in the UK is not the Answer' (2007) 70 (5) *Modern Law Review* 759.

It is argued, therefore, that the allegation that the Court adopts a generally unduly cautious approach is built upon a concept – that of apparently undue narrowness – that is too slippery to properly understand. There is no gauge, or baseline, within the literature as to how the Court should act in order to avoid the label of undue caution. The Court's approach is that if it has (at least) a real, or lurking, doubt about the conviction the appeal will be allowed; otherwise it will be dismissed. It is unclear why such an approach ought to be considered unduly cautious, given that it is the Court that heard the appeal, reviewed the evidence, and received submissions from counsel on both sides. Whilst it may be possible to point to particular cases with which one disagrees, on the basis of alleged narrowness or otherwise, that does not evidence an unduly cautious approach in general. Indeed, even if it can be shown that the Court's decision was wrong in particular cases, that does not mean that the test is wrong, or that the Court's general application of it is wrong.

It is submitted that talk of the Court's unduly cautious approach ought to be abandoned for the aforementioned reasons. If reform of the Court's powers is to be premised on the idea that the reform will correct an unduly cautious approach, when the Court does not accept that it has such an approach, and it is not clear what such an approach means in practice, that reform will be bound to fail. It is likely that this is why previous reforms in the same direction also failed; the Court was being asked to change an approach it did not recognise in its ordinary decision-making. It will be argued in Chapter 2 that there is a more substantial concept – risk – that can better illuminate the Court's processes and provide a more solid foundation; it can move the debate forward and provide a stronger foundation for reform. Sustained discussion of the concept of risk as it related to appeals against conviction is found in Chapter 2.

Conclusion

The Court of Appeal has exercised the unsafety test since the enactment of the Criminal appeal Act 1995. The test was enacted in response to sustained criticism of the Court's approach, the supposition being that the Court's approach is too cautious. That view has been challenged as lacking a clear theoretical foundation. The unsafety test is a broad and inchoate test, with no clear boundaries and so the Court's approach towards that test is central. If it cannot be properly said that the Court's approach is actually *unduly* cautious any attempt to remedy such an approach will fail, in the same way as previous attempts to remedy the apparent approach have, ostensibly, failed. Consequently, a better concept is needed, a concept that more clearly aligns with the Court's practices and takes better account of the conditions in which appeals against conviction are heard. The concept of risk and the tolerance thereof satisfies these requirements and provides a robust and suitable lens to evaluate the Court's decision-making. Chapter 2 explores the concept in detail.

References

Associated Provincial Pictures Houses Ltd v Wednesbury Corp [1948] 1 KB 223

Auld, R, *Review of the Criminal Courts of England and Wales* (HMSO, 2001)

Bingham, T, 'Justice and Injustice' in Bingham, T, (ed), *The Business of Judging* (Oxford University Press, 2000) 296

Cohen, F E, 'Transcendental Nonsense and the Functional Approach' (1935) 35 (6) *Columbia Law Review* 809

Court of Appeal, *Annual Report 2019–2020*, https://www.judiciary.uk/wp-content/uploads/2022/07/6.7429_JO_Court_of_Appeal_Criminalwillbet.pdf

Court of Appeal, *Annual Report 2022–2023*, https://www.judiciary.uk/wp-content/uploads/2024/07/24.16_JO_A_Review_of_the_Year_In_the_Court_of_Appeal_Criminal_Division_2022-23_WEB.pdf

Court of Appeal, *Annual Report 2023–2024*, https://www.judiciary.uk/wp-content/uploads/2025/01/24.278_JO_A_Review_of_the_Year_In_the_Court_of_Appeal_Criminal_Division_2023-24_WEB.pdf

Courts Act 2003

Criminal Appeal Act 1968

Criminal Procedure Rules

Darbyshire, P, *Sitting in Judgment: The Working Lives of Judges* (Hart, 2011)

Dargue, P, 'The Safety of Convictions in the Court of Appeal: Fresh Evidence in the Criminal Division through an Empirical Lens' (2019) 83 (6) *Journal of Criminal Law* 433

Dargue, P, 'The Tolerability of Risk in the Court of Appeal (Criminal Division): An Empirical Study of Appeals against Conviction 2015–2021' (2025) *Criminal Law Review* 743

Hart, H L A, *The Concept of Law* (3rd edn, Oxford University Press, 2012)

Home Office, *Papers Relating to the Case of George Edalji* (Cd. 3503, 1907)

Justice, *Criminal Appeals* (Stevens and Sons, 1964)

Justice Committee 12th Report of Session 2014–15, *Criminal Cases Review Commission* (2015 HC 850)

Knight, M, *Criminal Appeals* (Stevens and Sons, 1970

Law Commission, *Criminal Appeals: Consultation Paper* (Law Comm No 268, 2025)

Lord Chancellor's Office, Interdepartmental Committee on the Court of Criminal Appeal, *Report* (1965 Cmnd 2755)

Malleson, K, *The Royal Commission on Criminal Justice Research Study No 17* (HMSO, 1993)

McCartney, C, Roberts, S, 'Building Institutions to Address Miscarriages of Justice in England and Wales: "Mission Accomplished?"' (2013) 80 (4) *University of Cincinnati Law Review* 1333

Mullin, C, *Error of Judgment: The Truth about the Birmingham Bombings* (Poolbeg Press, 1990)

Naughton, M, *The Innocent and the Criminal Justice System: A Sociological Analysis of Miscarriages of Justice* (Palgrave MacMillan, 2013)

Nobles, R, *Understanding Miscarriages of Justice: The Law, The Media, and the Inevitability of Crisis* (Oxford University Press, 2000)

Nobles, R, Schiff, D, 'The Never Ending Story: Disguising Tragic Choices in Criminal Justice' (1997) 60 (2) *Modern Law Review* 293

Parl Deb HC 29 July 1907
Pattenden, R, *English Criminal Appeals 1844–1994* (Clarendon Press, 1996)
R v Allen (1909) 1 Cr App R 18
R v Al-Shumari [2025] EWCA Crim 1317
R v BOB [2024] EWCA Crim 1494
R v Castree [2008] EWCA Crim 1866
R v CCRC ex parte Pearson [2000] 1 Cr App R 141
R v Cooper (1969) 53 Cr App R 82
R v D [2013] EWCA Crim 1592
R v Davis, Rowe, and Johnson [2001] 1 Cr App R 8
R v Erskine [2009] EWCA Crim 1425
R v Hanson and others [2005] EWCA Crim 824
R v Kiszko (1979) 68 Cr App R 62
R v Laws 1 Cr App R 6
R v Lee (1909) 1 Cr App R 5
R v Lewis (1938) 26 Cr App R 110
R v Lucas (1981) 73 Cr App R 159
R v Malkinson [2006] EWCA Crim 1891
R v Malkinson [2023] EWCA Crim 954
R v McIlkenny and others (1991) 93 Cr App R 28
R v Osborne (1909) 1 Cr App R 144
R v Pendleton [2001] UKHL 66
R v Pope [2012] EWCA Crim 2241
R v Simpson (1909) 2 Cr App R 128
R v Stafford and Luvaglio [1974] AC 878
R v W [2022] EWCA Crim 1438
Roberts, P, Zuckerman, A, *Roberts and Zuckerman's Criminal Evidence* (3rd edn, Oxford University Press, 2022)
Roberts, S, 'Fresh Evidence and Factual Innocence in the Criminal Division of the Court of Appeal' (2017) 81 (4) *Criminal Law Review* 304
Roberts, S, 'Reviewing the Function of the Criminal Appeals in England and Wales' (2017) 1 *Institute of Law Journal* 1
Ross, R E, *The Court of Criminal Appeal* (Butterwort and Co., 1911)
Royal Commission on Criminal Justice, *Report* (Cm 2263, 1993)
Seabourne Davies, D, 'The Court of Criminal Appeal: The First Forty Years' (1951) 1 *Journal of the Society of Public Teachers of Law* (N.S) 425
Smith, J, 'The Criminal Appeal Act 1995: Part 1: Appeals against Conviction' (1995) *Criminal Law Review* 920
Stephen, J, *A Digest on the Law of Evidence* (5th edn, 1887)
Taylor, P, *Taylor on Criminal Appeals* (3rd edn, Oxford University Press, 2022)

2 Uncertainty, unsafety, and risk

Introduction

The Court of Appeal (Criminal Division) sits atop the wider criminal justice system in a reviewing capacity. In light of the Law Commission's ongoing consultation into the criminal appeal system there is a realistic prospect of reform in the future. If reform is premised on the notion of correcting an unduly cautious approach when it is not clear that it can be said it has that approach that reform is destined to fail. It was argued in Chapter 1 that talk of an unduly narrow approach ought to be abandoned as not helpful. A better concept or theoretical framework is needed to provide a more sound basis for potential reform in the future. The concept of risk, and the assessment and tolerance thereof, better serves the task at hand: providing an accurate and more conceptually stable theoretical framework. The assessment of risk in ordinary life provides a gauge / standard to which the Court can be held and against which the Court's actual behaviour can be scrutinised.

The concept of risk better takes account of a number of factors that are important in the context of criminal appeals that have largely been neglected. Namely, risk as a concept helps to make sense of the problem of uncertainty and how decisions are taken under such conditions. This book is concerned with one relatively narrow and particular aspect of risk: those risks that arise in the criminal justice system, and the appeal system in particular. The Court does not talk in terms of risk or risk toleration, but it does talk in terms of safety, and there are strong normative links between the concepts of risk and safety. It is not suggested that the Court does actually conduct a conduct a risk assessment in its judgments. It is argued instead that the concept of risk and its relationship with the concept of safety / unsafety can cast significant light on the decision-making of the Court and its approach. Thus, risk and its assessment and toleration serve as an optimal lens and theoretical framework through which to observe the Court's decision-making with a view to reform.

DOI: 10.4324/9781003782292-3

Risk taking and the criminal process

As a noun, the word 'risk' has been said to have at least five different senses: a) an unwanted event that may or may not occur; b) the cause of an unwanted event that may or may not occur; c) the probability of an unwanted event that may or may not occur; d) the statistical expected value of an unwanted event that may or may not occur; and e) the fact that a decision is made under conditions of known probabilities.[1] As a verb, 'to risk' means to 'expose to danger or loss' or to 'act in such a way as to incur risk'.[2] Trimpop defined risk taking behaviour as 'any consciously, or non-consciously controlled behaviour with a perceived uncertainty about its outcome, and / or about its possible benefits for . . . oneself or others'.[3] A risk was further described by Kates as being 'an uncertain consequence of an event or activity with respect to something humans value'.[4] As can be seen, every conception of risk requires that there is uncertainty about the outcomes of prospective actions.[5]

It will be observed that of the five different senses of risk referred to here, the first two are non-probabilistic and the latter three refer to probabilities. Probability is thus central to risk; probabilities are numbers between zero and one that attach to certain types of propositions; if an event cannot occur then its probability is zero, while if an event is certain to occur its probability is one. It will be discussed in further detail, but for the present discussion a risk can be calculated on probabilistic terms by taking the probability that some unwanted outcome will occur, or, alternatively, by taking the probability that some unwanted outcome will occur and multiplying it by the severity of the harm.[6] On the first interpretation, if two unwanted outcomes are assessed as being one-in-a-million events, they are equally risky even if the harm engaged in one is trivial and the other is fatal. On the second interpretation, if two unwanted outcomes are one-in-a-million but one is fatal and one is trivial, the former is more risky than the latter. It is submitted that the second measurement is more relevant to criminal appeals.

There are two general main schools of thought with regard to probability and the imposition of risk: the subjective and the objective.[7] In the objective

1 See M Boholm, N Moller, S O Hansson, 'The Concepts of Risk, Safety, and Security: Applications in Everyday Language' (2016) 36 (2) *Risk Analysis* 320, 321.

2 *Concise Oxford English Dictionary* (11th edn, Oxford University Press, 2008).

3 R M Trimpop, *The Psychology of Risk Taking Behaviour* (Elsevier, 1994) 9.

4 R W Kates, C Hohenemser, J Kasperson, *Perilous Progress: Managing the Hazards of Technology* (Westview Press, 1985) 21.

5 J F Yates, E R Stone, 'The Risk Construct' in J F Yates (ed), *Risk-Taking Behaviour* (John Wiley and Sons, 1992) 11.

6 For interesting discussion see J Oberdiek, *Imposing Risk: A Normative Framework* (Oxford University Press, 2017) 16–17.

7 See N Fenton, D Lagnado, 'Bayesianism: Objections and Rebuttals' in C Dahlman, A Stein, G Tuzet (eds), *Philosophical Foundations of Evidence Law* (Oxford University Press, 2021).

approach, probabilities are said to reflect reality and are based on empirically estimable relative frequencies.[8] Thus, if the probability of a random student being a bassoon-historian is 1/500, the relative frequency of bassoon-historians amongst students is 1/500.[9] The relative 'risk', therefore, of finding a bassoon-historian student is 1/500. The problem with the frequency analysis is that the probability of a particular student being a bassoon-historian will not be the same as the general frequency of bassoon-historians amongst the general student population; if a particular student is a bassoon-player there may well be a greater than 1/500 chance that she is also a bassoon-historian.[10] What matters is not objective frequency but the facts as they apply to a particular person.

As to subjective conceptions of probability (e.g. Bayesian), probability is defined as the degree of belief of a particular individual.[11] The thesis is that people's personal probabilities will converge once their available probability estimates are constrained by additional evidence.[12] It suggests that there is no one 'true' probability out there. The basic Bayesian procedure is that the investigator assigns a probability to a particular event in advance of any evidence, which is then subsequently updated by the addition of further evidence.[13] For instance, the probability of it raining tomorrow is assessed subjectively by the presence of dark clouds and a rising barometer. That assessment would likely converge around a similar range for most people properly (rationally) taking account of the evidence. The conclusion, which it is plausible to think that everybody considering the same evidence would reach, can be considered subjective.[14]

When there is a possibility of an unwanted outcome, there is a risk. As Oberdiek said, risk 'involves subjecting one or more people to some probability that they will suffer a setback to their interests'.[15] In the context of criminal appeals, as will be discussed, the appellants who appear before it could have been wrongfully convicted. It cannot be reasonably expected that the Court correctly locates all the innocent; that would be a level of perfection not demanded elsewhere in society (see the following). How much risk the Court should be prepared to tolerate is the core concern of the remainder of this chapter. The Court has two options (to allow or dismiss the appeal), and both impose a risk. Reaching a wrong result would be a serious setback to the interests of an appellant or the respondent prosecution. But the risk must be

8 J Cohen, *An Introduction to the Philosophy of Induction and Probability* (Oxford University Press, 1989) 47.
9 J Cohen, *An Introduction to the Philosophy of Induction and Probability* (Oxford University Press, 1989) 47–48.
10 J Cohen, *An Introduction to the Philosophy of Induction and Probability* (Oxford University Press, 1989) 48–49.
11 D Gillies, *Philosophical Theories of Probability* (Routledge, 2000) 53.
12 Cohen (n 8) 67.
13 Cohen (n 8) 68.
14 Gillies (n 11) 69.
15 Oberdiek (n 6) 17.

taken, because the Court must provide an answer to the question of whether a conviction is safe or unsafe.

The criminal process takes place under conditions of uncertainty, whereby the decisions made in the process carry uncertain consequences in respect of something that humans value; namely, the doing of justice. Almost every action humans take has uncertain consequences because the future cannot be foreseen; such actions are inherently risky and the agent is risk taking. Risk can be calculated, controlled, and sought to be reduced, but can never be extinguished other than by ceasing to do the action in question. When the risky action is something discretionary – for instance, sky diving – that is easily done; one can simply stop sky diving if one finds it too risky. When the risk is relatively trivial and transient, say, the risk of getting wet if one goes out without a coat, it is not worth expending too much effort trying to reduce the risk any further. But it is not always possible to avoid taking risks. Driving to work on a morning is risky. In 2024 there were 128,272 casualties of all severities, including 1602 fatalities, on the roads in Great Britain.[16] However, it is not easy to avoid driving to work if one's survival depends upon the drawing of a salary or the earning of a wage. Furthermore, even if one is embarking upon, ostensibly, the most risk free activity, such as sitting quietly at home watching television, there remains risk. The television may spark an electrical fire, one may have a heart attack alone, or the roof could cave in. It is, therefore, not possible to extinguish all risk.

The criminal process

The most significant problem of uncertainty for the criminal justice system is this one: the question 'is the defendant guilty?' is forever uncertain.[17] It cannot be said with mathematical certainty that a suspect is guilty. This uncertainty exists because time cannot be reversed, and it cannot be seen exactly what happened and why during an alleged event at some point in the (possibly distant) past. The task is made more difficult still because most criminal offences require not only that the defendant committed the act (the *actus reus*) but also that she had the necessary *mens rea.* If it was possible to find some way to say with certainty that the defendant was guilty, the system would surely do that. If that could be done, the expensive, time-consuming, and stressful fact-finding parts of the criminal process would not be necessary.

Since mathematical certainty of guilt is not possible, there is in every case room for doubt and so the possibility of mistake. Sometimes the possibility

16 UK Government, https://www.gov.uk/government/statistics/reported-road-casualties-great-britain-annual-report-2024/reported-road-casualties-great-britain-annual-report-2024#overall-casualties-and-rates.

17 D V Lindley, *Understanding Uncertainty, Revised Edition* (John Wiley & Sons, 2014) 1.3.

of having made a mistake appears remote. For instance, where a crime is committed in broad daylight, with numerous witnesses, no plausible defence, and where the perpetrators repeatedly admit to having committed the crime on television.[18] But one cannot be mathematically certain with a probability of 1 of guilt. The time may come at some point in the future where there is doubt raised about a perpetrator's guilt. While doubt might appear remote at one particular point in time, it is remains a possibility and so this prevents being able to say with certainty that a person is guilty. While doubts can exist, it should be noted that some doubts can be too remote to prevent a finding of guilt, because the process sets a standard of proof below certainty.

It will be noticed that the problem of uncertainty abuts the rather dogmatic and absolutist terms of the overriding objective to deal with cases justly. The overriding objective states that dealing with cases justly includes achieving factually correct outcomes: acquitting the innocent and convicting the guilty. Obtaining accuracy is thus the basic epistemic idea of the criminal process.[19] In more formal terms the logic behind the criminal process is that the primary aim of fact finding in the criminal process is finding the truth about facts; that the truth can be found through inductive logic; truth is an objective truth corresponding to reality; and that justice is the correct application of substantive law to true facts.[20] This view maintains a correspondence theory of truth, whereby something is true if it corresponds to some fact, it is then the duty of the criminal justice system to locate it. There is, thus, a 'fundamental epistemological assumption that, in principle, the truth about past events and present states of affairs is capable of being inferred from evidence'.[21]

The most important part of the criminal process for the purposes of this book, apart from the appeal system, is the trial. At trial there is a 'trade-off between procedures that maximise the chances of convicting the guilty, and those that maximise the chances of acquitting the innocent'.[22] As such, it can be said that there is no demand to always reach the right decision; the demand is that the risk is properly apportioned.

18 The case which comes to mind is the 2014 murder of Lee Rigby, see Intelligence and Security Committee, *Report on the Intelligence Relating to the Murder of Fusilier Lee Rigby* (HC 795, 2014). The perpetrators did apply for permission to appeal against conviction and sentence, but permission was refused as being 'completely hopeless': *R v Adebolajo; Adebowale* [2014] EWCA Crim 2779 [33].

19 A Stein, *Foundations of Evidence Law* (Oxford University Press, 2005) 12.

20 See W Twining, *Rethinking Evidence: Exploratory Essays* (2nd edn, Cambridge University Press, 2006) 103. See also W Twining, 'Some Scepticism about Some Scepticisms' (1984) 11 *Journal of Law and Society* 137. For a counter see D Nicholson, 'Taking Epistemology Seriously: "Truth, Reason and Justice" Revisited' (2013) 17 (1) *International Journal of Evidence and Proof* 1.

21 I Dennis, *The Law of Evidence* (8th edn, Oxford University Press, 2024) 156.

22 Dennis (n 21) 160, citing A Sanders, 'Core Values, the Magistracy, and the Auld Report' (2002) 29 (2) *Journal of Law and Society* 324, 325.

The trial

In the year ending September 2025, 78,000 defendants appeared for trial at a Crown Court in England and Wales.[23] Of those, 12,000 (15%) pleaded not guilty, requiring a trial.[24] In the end, 4300 (36%) of those were acquitted, and 7600 (64%) convicted by the jury.[25] If a risk is as an uncertain consequence of an event or activity with respect to something humans value, then subjecting a person to trial is surely a risk. The 'something' that humans value is the doing of justice. As noted, key to dealing with cases justly is achieving accuracy: acquitting the innocent and convicting the guilty. Both these outcomes are outcomes that humans value. The former is valued because the imposition of punishment can never be just if it is against the innocent; it is instead a miscarriage of justice. The latter is valued because the purpose of the criminal law is to 'announce to society that these actions are not to be done and to secure that fewer of them are done'.[26] Thus, despite the risk that is involved in a trial, it is considered worth the risk in order to achieve justice by having a chance to convict the guilty.

The jury determines facts, and so its chief responsibility is to convict the guilty and acquit the innocent. The factual (epistemic) consequences of a trial are often presented by a schematic such as this one (Table 2.1):

Table 2.1 Schematic of trial outcomes

Wanted outcomes	*Unwanted outcomes*
True convictions (true positive)	False convictions (false positive)
True acquittals (true negative)	False acquittals (false negative)

This serves as a reminder that the jury can produce wanted outcomes and convict the guilty (true positives) and acquit the innocent (true negatives). But the trial risks the production of unwanted outcomes: the conviction of the innocent (false positives) and acquittal of the guilty (false negatives). The problem of uncertainty means that it cannot be known which of the defendants on trial are truly guilty; in trying to achieve the wanted outcomes of correct verdicts, there is the risk of procuring the unwanted outcomes. The unwanted outcomes, acquittal of the guilty and conviction of the innocent, are not equally deleterious to the doing of justice and so are not sought to be avoided

23 See Ministry of Justice, https://www.gov.uk/government/statistics/criminal-justice-statistics-quarterly-september-2025, overview tables, Q3.1.

24 This statistic was achieved using the 'Crown Court Data Tool: September 2025' on the prior link.

25 Figures do not sum due to rounding.

26 H L A Hart, 'Prolegomenon to the Principles of Punishment' in H L A Hart (ed), *Punishment and Responsibility* (2nd edn, Oxford University Press, 2008) 6.

with equal strength. In a normative sense, the conviction of the innocent is significantly worse than the acquittal of the guilty.

A trial is an important normative moment: 'a unique and essentially unrepeatable public event' in which the critical eye of the layman, and his sense of justice, authenticates that the proper processes have been observed.[27] The whole of England and Wales cannot sit together to determine whether or not a defendant on trial is guilty, and so the task is delegated to a small section of the local community. For the more serious criminal offences tried in Crown Courts that is the jury. Jurors will swear an oath to faithfully try the defendant and reach a true verdict according to the evidence. The law of evidence will govern which evidence is to be put before them. The defendant might adduce evidence in an attempt to rebut the prosecution's case, or he might adduce no evidence and say nothing at all. The trial judge will summarise the case and direct the jury on the law and how to approach their task.

Although the trial is an unique and consequential public moment in time, it is not perfect. Rawls described it as being an example of imperfect procedural justice because 'while there is an independent criterion for the correct outcome, there is no feasible procedure which is sure to lead to it'.[28] The trial is a presentation of the facts through advocates (who have their own professional obligations),[29] fading memories, and rules of evidence. That presentation may be further distorted by lies, false memory, or simple mistake.[30] This, and the fundamental problem of uncertainty, is why the risk of unwanted outcome arises. Since there is significant social value (the doing of justice by convicting the guilty) it is evidently a risk that is considered worth taking (there has been no major clamouring for the abolition of the criminal trial), so long as that risk is apportioned in the right direction.[31] The key mechanism for the apportionment of that risk at trial is the standard of proof, which apportions the risk in favour of suspects and defendants.

There is a long and enduring principle that the risks taken at trial should be apportioned to favour defendants. The risk is apportioned in this way because nothing can normatively justify the conviction of the innocent. The conviction of the innocent must be a miscarriage of justice; a 'failure to attain the desired end result of justice'.[32] Nothing can normatively justify the conviction of the

27 P Roberts, A Zuckerman, *Roberts and Zuckerman's Criminal Evidence* (3rd edn, Oxford University Press, 2022) 100.

28 J Rawls, *A Theory of Justice Revised Edition* (Harvard University Press, 1999) 74–75.

29 Such as not to mislead the Court, and to fearlessly represent their client, whether the prosecution and the defence. See Bar Standards Board, *Handbook* (BSB, 2026).

30 See eg T Hillier, G Dingwall, *Criminal Justice and the Pursuit of Truth* (Bristol University Press, 2021).

31 Stein (n 19) 13.

32 C Walker, 'Miscarriages of Justice in Principle and Practice' in C Walker, K Starmer (eds), *Miscarriages of Justice: A Review of Justice in Error* (Oxford University Press, 1999) 31.

innocent principally because upon conviction a person is liable to be punished. Punishment is difficult enough to justify against the guilty, because it is the intentional infliction of harm by the state against its own citizens; which is the opposite of what states are supposed to do.[33]

It is, however, possible to justify the acquittal of the guilty. Being prepared to acquit some of the guilty, by making it difficult to traverse the criminal process and be convicted if the defendant denies liability, makes it more likely that any innocents will be successfully acquitted as well. Moreover, the terms of the overriding objective mean that it may on occasion be just to acquit the guilty. The overriding objective requires that both sides are treated fairly, and that the defendant's rights under Article 6 of the European Convention on Human Rights are observed. If fairness is itself a condition of justice, upholding a conviction of the guilty that was obtained by unfair means would constitute an injustice despite its being factually accurate. The House of Lords in *Horseferry Road Magistrates ex parte Bennett* accepted on behalf of the judiciary the role of overseeing executive action and refusal to countenance 'behaviour that threatens basic human rights or the rule of law'.[34]

Despite this preference for apportioning risk towards affording protection to suspects, the trial does not do everything it could do to protect them. As Dennis said, in setting the level of accuracy required for conviction, 'the costs of acquitting the guilty cannot be ignored'.[35] Although convicting the innocent is an unwanted outcome, acquitting the guilty is as well, for both would represent prima facie failure of the overriding objective of dealing with cases justly. Moreover, the more difficult it is made to convict anybody, the greater the risk of acquitting a person who is guilty.[36] It could be made more difficult to convict anybody, in order to protect any innocents who are on trial, by tightening the conditions necessary for a guilty verdict to be returned. Straightforward refinements could be, for instance, to outlaw the use of bad character evidence, hearsay, and inferences from silence. But the most impactful thing that could be done, if it was desired to further protect the innocent, would be to alter the standard of proof to something even higher than it currently is.

The standard of proof at trial is that the prosecution must prove guilt 'beyond reasonable doubt'. The Crown Court Compendium provides that the judge should direct juries that: 'if, after considering all of the evidence, you are sure that D is guilty, your verdict must be guilty. If you are not sure that D

33 As per Bentham: 'punishment, whatever shape it may assume, is an evil' (J Bentham, *The Rationale of Punishment* (Robert Heward, 1830). See also V Tadros, *The Ends of Harm: The Moral Foundations of Criminal Law* (Oxford University Press, 2011) chapter 1.

34 [1994] 1 AC 42.

35 Dennis (n 21) 160.

36 Dennis (n 21) 160.

is guilty, your verdict must be not guilty'.[37] Whether this is any clearer than 'beyond a reasonable doubt' is debatable.[38] A recent study by McKeown and his colleagues found that 75.5% of survey respondents believed that being 'sure' of guilt meant being *absolutely certain* of guilt.[39] But if 'certain' is taken to mean mathematical (formal) certainty,[40] then that answer cannot be right. The 'correct' answer to the meaning of sure must be *very highly probable,* or one notch below formal certainty, an answer given by only 12% of survey respondents.[41]

Standards of proof 'express policy choices about how to resolve uncertainty in light of two related, primary considerations: accuracy and allocating the risk of error between the parties'.[42] While the standard of proof does have this aim, there is a dispute as to the processes that are involved. On one view, the 'probabilistic' view, the question at trial is whether *X* or *not-X* is more probable, under the other view (relative plausibility) the question is whether X or Y is more plausible.[43] On the probability account, the beyond reasonable doubt standard is a probability of (approximately) 0.9 or greater, and guilt is proven if the probability of guilt exceeds that threshold with the evidence contributing for or against that threshold in a quantitative manner.[44] A pure probabilistic account, however, does not provide any feasible way of quantifying evidence, and is inconsistent with how judges and juries actually evaluate evidence.[45] The relative plausibility approach, like the probability approach, aims to assess the likelihood of disputed facts, but through the evaluation of the relative plausibility of the contrasting explanations.[46] When the standard is beyond reasonable doubt, the jury can only convict

37 *Crown Court Compendium* (Part 1) 2025, Chapter 5–3.

38 P McKeown, A Keane, S Stares, 'Comprehension of "Sure" as the Description of the Criminal Standard of Proof: An Empirical Study' (2025) 9 *Criminal Law Review* 518; P McKeown, 'The Crown Court Compendium and the Criminal Standard of Proof: Suggestions to aid Juror Comprehension and Help Judges' (2022) 11 *Criminal Law Review* 893; A Keane, 'Not So Sure About the Criminal Standard of Proof' (2020) 170 (7898) *New Law Journal* 15; M Zander, 'The Criminal Standard of Proof: How Sure Is Sure?' (2000) 150 (1517) *New Law Journal* 18.

39 McKeown (n 38) 'Comprehension' 527.

40 It is plausible that when answering that 'sure' means 'certain' respondents were referring to moral certainty, not mathematical certainty, see C N Heffer, 'The Language of Conviction and the Convictions of Certainty: Is "Sure" an Impossible Standard of Proof?' (2007) 5 (1) *International Commentary on Evidence* i.

41 McKeown (n 38) 'Comprehension' 527.

42 R J Allen, M S Pardo, 'Relative Plausibility and Its Critics' (2019) 23 *International Journal of Evidence and Proof* 5, 9–10.

43 See Allen and Pardo (n 42) fn6. See also A Biederman, D Caruso, K N Kotsoglou, 'Decision Theory, Relative Plausibility and the Criminal Standard of Proof' (2021) 15 *Criminal Law and Philosophy* 131.

44 Allen and Pardo (n 42) 11.

45 Allen and Pardo (n 42) 14.

46 Allen and Pardo (n 42) 15.

when the prosecution's explanation is plausible and there is no plausible defence explanation.[47] 'Legal fact-finders arrive at probabilistic conclusions by evaluating and comparing the plausibility of explanations'.[48] This view of adjudication seems to overcome some of the weaknesses of the probability approach.[49]

Whatever the precise mechanisms, the standard of proof protects from conviction where there is evidenced, and so reasonable, doubt about guilt; it does not provide protection where there is un-evidenced (even if true) doubt about guilt.[50] A clear exposition of such is provided by Denning J (as he then was) in *Miller v Minister of Pensions*.[51] Explaining the meaning of beyond reasonable doubt in a non-criminal context, he said the cogency 'need not reach certainty but does not mean proof beyond the shadow of a doubt', because:

> The law would fail to protect the community if it admitted fanciful possibilities to deflect the course of justice. If the evidence is so strong against a man as to leave only a remote possibility in his favour which can be dismissed with the sentence "of course it is possible, but not in the least probable", the case is proved beyond reasonable doubt, but nothing short of that will suffice.

The standard of proof in the criminal trial is sufficiently high that where there is evidenced doubt / plausible doubt about guilt the defendant must be acquitted (even if guilty) but sufficiently low that conviction is possible. It is against this background that the Court sits in review of the criminal process and especially the trial. The legislature has provided that the Court is to step in whenever it (the Court) thinks that a conviction rendered under these conditions is unsafe. Thus, the relationship between the concept of risks taken and the concept of safety needs some elaboration. When the unsafety test is seen in the context of its relation to risk the functions of the Court as protecting from unacceptable risk become clearer and can be made explicit.

Risk and (un)safety

Amongst the 7600 defendants convicted by a jury in the year ending 2025 there will be some that were not treated justly: some persons will be wrongly convicted, in particular some innocents will be convicted. The problem is

47 Allen and Pardo (n 42) 16.
48 Allen and Pardo (n 42) 21.
49 Allen and Pardo (n 42) 17–19.
50 Stein (n 19) chapter 6.
51 [1947] 2 All ER 372.

that it is impossible to know how many, and more importantly: which, of the convicted defendants were the wrongly convicted. It must be the case that each year some percentage of convicted defendants will be innocent. Whether in a given year that was less than 1%, or whether it was 100% is unknowable, and attempts to compute a reasonable estimate are unconvincing.[52] This is an example of a reference class problem, in which the probability of a single event (e.g. 'wrongful conviction') changes depending upon how it is classified.[53] What is known for sure, however, is that some convicted people do submit an application for permission to appeal, some are granted permission, and some appeals are allowed due to being unsafe and some dismissed due to being safe.

It is reasonable to assume that amongst the persons who do appeal there will be some innocents (all of whom are by definition wrongly convicted) and some guilty (some of whom will be rightly and properly convicted, and some of whom will be wrongly convicted). But the problem of uncertainty means that no particular individual can be reliably placed into one of these categories over another. Appellants who should have their convictions quashed are, therefore, placed at risk of not having their convictions quashed. While is this unfortunate, it is a product of the problem of uncertainty and it cannot reasonably be asserted that the Court should guarantee all wrongful convictions are remedied. The legislature has directed the Court to place appellants (or rather, their convictions) into two categories delineated by whether they are safe or unsafe. The risk is, therefore, apportioned. Recourse to the concept of risk and safety in a more general sense helps to ascertain how much risk should be entertained.

Atkins identified three senses of the word 'safety': a) the condition of not being in danger; b) the quality of not being dangerous, and c) a place where there is safety from a particular danger.[54] In safety management, something is considered to be safe when there is '*freedom from unacceptable outcomes or from unacceptable risks*'.[55] There is thus an unextractable link between the concepts of risk and safety. Since something can be considered safe when there is freedom from unacceptable risk, it follows that some risk can be acceptable given the right circumstances. As Renn said, 'a risk can be considered tolerable

52 It is unconvincing because, at the end of the day, it is simply impossible to know so all attempts are simply educated guesses, see S R Gross, B O'Brien, 'Frequency and Predictors of False Conviction: Why We Know So Little, and New Data on Capital Cases' (2008) 5 (4) *Journal of Empirical Legal Studies* 927. See also S Gross, 'How Many False Convictions Are There? How Many Exonerations Are There?' in C R Huff, M Killias (eds), *Wrongful Convictions and Miscarriages of Justice* (Routledge, 2013).

53 See A Hájek, 'The Reference Class Problem Is Your Problem Too' (2007) 156 (3) *Synthese* 563.

54 B T S Atkins, 'Building a Lexicon: The Contribution of Lexicography' (1991) 4 (3) *International Journal of Lexicography* 167, 169–172.

55 H A Oltedal, 'Setting the Scene for Maritime Safety Management' in H A Oltedal, M Lützhöft (eds), *Managing Maritime Safety* (Routledge, 2018) 7.

when the activity is seen as worth pursuing for the benefit it carries yet requires additional effort for risk reduction within reasonable limits'.[56] This definition of safety maps closely onto the preceding discussion around the apportionment of risk which takes place in the criminal trial. The risk that is involved is apportioned to provide a protective element to the defendant, but the residual risk is tolerated due to the benefits that a trial brings. That risk is reduced to reasonable limits by the burden and standard of proof. Therefore, it is 'safe' to hold a trial and to convict a person, provided the efforts at risk reduction were properly observed.

Whether something is sufficiently safe to be doing can be determined by conducting a risk assessment. This is normally done by a cost-benefit analysis to determine whether the risks involved are worth the benefits of taking that risk.[57] As mentioned earlier, risk can be assessed through consideration of the likelihood of the unwanted event occurring and the severity of the loss should unwanted outcomes occur.[58] In quantitative risk analysis one can multiply the likelihood of harm occurring (as a percentage, such as a 10% chance of death) by the severity of the harm (such as the monetary amount an insurance company would need to pay on death) to give a measure of risk.[59] Risk assessment can also be conducted qualitatively by completing a table such as the following (Table 2.2):[60]

Table 2.2 Qualitative Risk Assessment Framework

Severity	*Likelihood of unwanted outcome*				
	Very unlikely	*Unlikely*	*Likely*	*Very likely*	*Almost certain*
Trivial	Very low (1)	Low	Low	Medium	Medium
Minor	Low	Low	Medium	Medium	Medium
Serious	Low	Medium	Medium (2)	Medium	High
Very serious	Medium	Medium	Medium	High	High
Fatal	Medium	Medium	High	High	Very high (3)

This maps the severity / seriousness of an unwanted outcome should it occur, against the likelihood of that unwanted outcome to provide a risk rating. Thus, an unwanted outcome that is both trivial and very unlikely is very low risk (marked 1). An unwanted event that is serious and of medium likelihood is of

56 O Renn, 'The Risk Handling Chain' in F Bouder, D Salvin, R E Lofstedt (eds), *The Tolerability of Risk: A New Framework for Risk Management* (Earthscan, 2007) 38.

57 See Yates and Stone (n 5) 3.

58 T Boyle, *Health and Safety: Risk Management* (5th edn, Routledge, 2019) 10.

59 T Boyle, *Health and Safety: Risk Management* (5th edn, Routledge, 2019) 11.

60 Taken from T Boyle, *Health and Safety: Risk Management* (5th edn, Routledge, 2019) 32, table 5.4.

medium risk (2), and an unwanted outcome that is almost certain to occur and fatal (3) is of very high risk. The lower risk something is, then, the safer it is and the easier the residual risk is to tolerate. Something that is very low risk is a risk that is probably worth taking for granted and should require little consideration. But something that is very high risk would require significant benefits in order to consider doing. It is this conception of risk as being severity of harm *x* likelihood of occurrence that is most useful[61] as a theoretical framework of the unsafety test because the Court's two options (to allow / to dismiss the appeal) risk harms of inherently different severity (discussed in the following), and so the likelihood of harm takes on an increasingly important role.

Hastie and Dawes described decision-making under uncertainty as pausing at a fork in the road and choosing one path to reach a desired goal or to avoid an unpleasant outcome.[62] Whenever one has to make a decision at that fork one needs to consider the possible future outcomes of that course of action, and the consequences of those actions set against one's goals and objectives.[63] The idea of a fork in the road followed by active deliberation brings to mind the judicial process. In a recent case in the England and Wales Court of Protection,[64] Mr Justice Poole was tasked with deciding whether to permit spinal surgery, followed by a lengthy period of intensive care, to be conducted on an 18-year-old male who could not consent to medical treatment himself.[65] These kinds of decisions are in common the Court of Protection and based upon the question of what is in the best interests of the patient; they represent a classic fork in the road situation. In some particularly perceptive comments on risk, Poole J observed that:[66]

> The assessment of best interests includes, but is not limited to, consideration of the risks and benefits of proceeding with the planned treatment, and of not doing so . . . Decision-makers have to look forward and so have to deal with uncertainty. It is a frequent mistake to believe that if something goes wrong after a decision then the decision must have been wrong. If a decision-maker chooses option X over option Y because X has a 90% chance of success and Y has only a 50% chance of success, and X fails, it does not mean that they made the wrong choice. There is rarely a risk free option, and there certainly is not one [in this case]. Where there is risk, there is the possibility of a poor or even a fatal outcome, but risk is inevitable, in particular when the decision to be made is finely balanced.

61 Cf Oberdiek (n 6) chapter 1.

62 R Hastie, R M Dawes, *Rational Choice in an Uncertain World* (Sage, 2001) 25.

63 R Hastie, R M Dawes, *Rational Choice in an Uncertain World* (Sage, 2001) 26.

64 A court which makes decisions on behalf of those who lack capacity to make decisions relating to their health.

65 *Re RS (Best Interests: Surgery and Intensive Care)* [2025] EWCOP 38.

66 *Re RS (Best Interests: Surgery and Intensive Care)* [2025] EWCOP 38–42.

The surgery held significant risk, a mortality risk of perhaps 10 percent, to the patient as well as a number of other less significant risks.[67] The Court held it was in the patient's best interests to have the surgery despite the risk.[68] In an appeal against conviction in the Court of Appeal, the Court is paused at a fork in the road. It knows what the desired goal is: the doing of justice. But it does not know with certainty what it needs to do in order to achieve that goal. The result is that by trying to do justice there is a risk of doing injustice which must be either tolerable or not tolerable. Since risk toleration is a core concept, it is useful to briefly consider two bodies that also consider risk and risk toleration: the Parole Board and the Health and Safety Executive. Their toleration of risk can help us to understand what level of risk toleration in the Court of Appeal is acceptable.

Tolerable and intolerable risk – the Parole Board

The England and Wales Parole Board's role in the criminal justice system is to determine whether life-sentenced (and some other) prisoners are safe to be released following the end of their minimum terms.[69] Section 28(6)(b) of the Crime (Sentences) Act 1997 provides that the Parole Board can only direct release if it 'is satisfied that it is no longer necessary for the protection of the public that the prisoner should be confined'. Following an incident in which a high-profile prisoner (John Worboys) was released directly from Category A prison conditions while serving an indefinite sentence for public protection (IPP), a decision later overruled by the High Court as *Wednesbury* irrational,[70] the government conducted a root and branch review.[71] That recommended, amongst other things, that section 28 be amended to adopt a more precautionary approach in which prisoners convicted of the most serious offences would not be released unless there was evidence of low risk to the public.

That change was made by the Victims and Prisoners Act 2024 which inserted section 28ZA into the 1997 Act. It now states that the Parole Board must not be satisfied that it is no longer necessary to confine the prisoner unless the Board thinks there is a *no more than minimal risk* that the prisoner would commit further offences of serious harm (section 28ZA(3)) (emphasis added). This change reflected the government's stated goal that the primary role of the Parole Board is to protect the safety of the public.[72] Parole Board guidance[73] states that the Board should refuse to direct release

67 *Re RS (Best Interests: Surgery and Intensive Care)* [2025] EWCOP 45.
68 *Re RS (Best Interests: Surgery and Intensive Care)* [2025] EWCOP 52.
69 See UK Government, https://www.gov.uk/government/organisations/parole-board
70 *R (On the Application of DSD) v Parole Board for England and Wales* [2019] QB 285.
71 Ministry of Justice, *Root and Branch Review of the Parole System* (CP 654 2022).
72 Root and Branch Review (n 71) 76.
73 See Parole Board, *Types of Case Member Guidance* (Parole Board, 2023), https://www.gov.uk/government/publications/parole-board-types-of-cases-guidance-2023

when there is an unacceptable risk of serious violent or sexual offending,[74] and the enactment of section 28ZA can be taken to mean that 'unacceptable risk' is anything more than minimal.

It will be apparent that the decision as to risk by the Parole Board is taken under uncertain conditions and there is an apportionment of risk. At the time that the Board makes its decision, it cannot know whether a prisoner will re-offend or not; it cannot therefore always get its decisions right. The risks engaged are that the Board releases a prisoner who will commit further offences, or will decline to release (despite having served the punitive element of their sentence) a person who would not go on to offend.[75] It is clear from the statutory provisions that the risk apportionment is skewed heavily against the prisoner and away from release. Presumably this is because the prisoner, as a convicted person, has been 'proven' to be guilty of an offence and the decision to release would be a positive action by the Parole Board that creates a new risk to the public. One could observe that similar conditions apply in the Court of Appeal. Despite this risk there is a tolerable – albeit small – level of risk in the test for release. The Board is not required to be certain that the prisoner will not re-offend, but it cannot release if there is an unacceptable risk of re-offending.

The Parole Board has been directed by the legislature to have a low tolerance towards the risk of future offending, despite the fact that withholding parole might constitute injustice for a prisoner who would not re-offend. It is the right of Parliament to make that direction. It might be compared to the unsafety test. The unsafety test in the Criminal Appeal Act 1968 simply leaves the task of assessing the risks involved in its decision-making to the Court of Appeal; it does not direct that it have any particular level of tolerance for risk.[76] That said, the Criminal Procedure Rules and the Court's jurisprudence (which have not been reversed by Parliament) disclose that the unsafety test is protective of an appellant's rights. This does not suggest that the Court has a high tolerance for the risk of doing injustice through its decisions.

Health and Safety Executive (HSE)

The England and Wales Health and Safety Executive (HSE) is the regulator and overseer of employment health and safety regulation. Its 2001 document, *Reducing Risks, Protecting People,* introduced the Tolerability of Risk (TOR)

74 Member guidance (n 80) 3.8.

75 See C McKay, 'Predicting Risk in Criminal Procedure: Actuarial Tools, Algorithms, AI, and Judicial Decision-Making' (2020) 32 (1) *Current Issues in Criminal Justice* 22.

76 When Parliament considered doing so, by seeking to limit the ability of the Court to quash convictions for procedural irregularities it was widely criticised; see J R Spencer, 'Quashing Convictions for Procedural Irregularities' (2007) *Criminal Law Review* 835.

framework into its decision-making.[77] It observed that there are three 'pure' criteria for assessing risk: equity-based, utility-based, and technology-based.[78] Equity-based criteria starts with a premise that individuals have unconditional rights to a certain level of protection from risk above which no individual can be exposed. The problem with this approach is that if the risk does exceed that level it is unacceptable whatever the benefits.[79] Utility-based approaches compare the benefit of introducing a risk reducing measure (e.g. fewer accidents) against the cost of it. The utility approach may ignore ethical considerations – some activities should ethically not be done even if there would be utility in doing so. The technology approach reflects the idea that technology can be used to control risk, but this may ignore the balance between benefits and cost.

Its TOR framework sought to accommodate all three criteria. Thus, the TOR framework divides increasing levels of risk into three regions: the broadly acceptable region, the tolerable region, and the unacceptable region. Where a particular risk is regarded as unacceptable it is ruled out regardless of the benefits unless it can be modified or there are exceptional reasons.[80] Thus, the unacceptable region is governed by principles of equity. The HSE cites the banning of the use or production of 2-naphthylamine and lead as activities banned on the basis of unacceptable risk.[81] In the acceptable region are activities in which the risks are insignificant or adequately controlled and that no further risk reduction effort is necessary.[82]

The tolerable region contains risks which people are prepared to tolerate to secure certain benefits provided the nature of the risk is assessed and is as low as reasonably practicable (ALARP).[83] As to the crucial boundary between tolerable and unacceptable risks, the HSE stresses the impact of the risked event on individuals but also on society. An activity giving rise to a particularly high individual risk would also engender social concerns on equity grounds. At the same time, an activity with a low individual average risk of harm could be considered socially unacceptable.[84] As Bandle observed, designating a risk as tolerable does not mean that the risk is negligible or unimportant, but that the cost involved in seeking to reduce the risk further is not worth the benefit of the reduced risk.[85]

The HSE is concerned primarily with employment health and safety, which is principally governed by the Health and Safety at Work etc. Act 1974. The

77 HSE, *Reducing Risks, Protecting People: HSE Decision-Making Process* (HSE, 2001).
78 HSE, *Reducing Risks, Protecting People: HSE Decision-Making Process* (HSE, 2001) 40–41.
79 HSE, *Reducing Risks, Protecting People: HSE Decision-Making Process* (HSE, 2001) 41.
80 HSE, *Reducing Risks, Protecting People: HSE Decision-Making Process* (HSE, 2001) 42.
81 HSE, *Reducing Risks, Protecting People: HSE Decision-Making Process* (HSE, 2001) 51.
82 HSE, *Reducing Risks, Protecting People: HSE Decision-Making Process* (HSE, 2001) 43.
83 HSE, *Reducing Risks, Protecting People: HSE Decision-Making Process* (HSE, 2001) 43.
84 HSE, *Reducing Risks, Protecting People: HSE Decision-Making Process* (HSE, 2001) 46.
85 T Bandle, 'Tolerability of Risk: The Regulator's Story' in F Bouder, D Salvin, R E Lofstedt (eds), *The Tolerability of Risk: A New Framework for Risk Management* (Earthscan, 2007) 96.

HSE is therefore the overseer of systems designed to protect the life and limb of millions of workers in England and Wales. There is more than a passing resemblance between the role of the HSE and the role of the Court of Appeal as overseers of their respective systems. Both are principally concerned with the question of safety. Both can issue judicial or quasi-judicial decisions about the effectiveness of safety processes. Importantly, both are involved in assessing the level of risk in relation to something that humans value. There is a societal value to ensuring that workplaces are safe and accidents are kept ALARP. The social value in the Court's assessment of risk pertains to the doing of justice: the quashing of convictions that should be quashed and the upholding of convictions that should be upheld.

The standard which the HSE sets to employers is to reduce risks so they are ALARP. Whether a risk is ALARP is the central consideration as to how far it is necessary to go to pursue risk reduction.[86] It is clear that employers are not required to do more than is reasonably practicable to reduce risks but are to weigh the risk against the sacrifice needed to further reduce it. Spending £1million to avoid a few bruised knees would be disproportionate, but spending the same amount to avoid 150 deaths would not be.[87] If a risk is reduced to ALARP then the employees are protected from unacceptable risk and the employers have discharged their obligations to keep workers safe; it is not required that all risk is extinguished. If this is the standard of safety that is acceptable to an organisation such as the HSE charged with protecting the life and limb of millions of workers, then it seems an appropriate standard to require of the Court of Appeal, which also engages in the concept of safety. Therefore, the Court is to protect appellants from unacceptable risk, it does not need to protect from all risk, nor does it need to take steps that are more than reasonable to reduce the risk so they are lower than ALARP.

The ALARP standard in the Court of Appeal

The problem of uncertainty is a particularly acute one for the Court of Appeal. Appeals against conviction concern persons who have been 'proven' guilty, the appellant either having pleaded guilty or (more commonly) having been convicted by a jury. The Court of Appeal cannot know whether the appellant before them is guilty, but it does know that he has already traversed a lengthy process, at the end of which was sure he was guilty. Those earlier parts of the criminal process sought to apportion the risk of wrongful conviction in favour of the defendant, but was prepared to tolerate the residual risk of injustice

86 See J McQuaid, 'Historical Perspectives on the Tolerability of Risk' in *The Tolerability of Risk* (n 85) 90.

87 See J McQuaid, 'Historical Perspectives on the Tolerability of Risk' in *The Tolerability of Risk* (n 85) 90.

caused by continuing with the prosecution and taking the appellant to trial. Since the trial has already sought to make it difficult to convict anybody, it should follow that a defendant who has been convicted is unlikely to be innocent. As discussed earlier, to render a guilty verdict, guilt must be significantly more probable, or plausible, than innocence.

The Court of Appeal has two options available to it: to allow the appeal or to dismiss the appeal. When the appeal is dismissed the situation is left to stand as it presently is; the appellant remains convicted and so subject to (continued) punishment. Since there is always a risk of a trial convicting an innocent, dismissing an appeal gives rise to the risk of upholding the conviction of the innocent; this is unwanted, but it is difficult to see how that risk could be extinguished altogether. If the appeal is allowed, the Court has stepped in and changed the record regarding that particular case. That gives rise to the risk that the Court will allow an appeal that did not need to be allowed. As Spencer observed over 40 years ago, the Court is particularly loath to act in a way that creates (what it sees as) an injustice where there was not one before.[88] What is the Court of Appeal to do when faced with an appellant who has been convicted by a jury which believed the prosecution's version of events and disbelieved the defendant's? How much protection should it be expected to extend to such a person? The Law Commission affirmed that the appellant should have the benefit of the apportionment of risk:

> The trial process is designed to prioritise acquittal of the innocent over conviction of the guilty: the former is considered a better outcome than the latter. The appeals system should reflect a similar principle, that if there is doubt about the safety of a conviction, the conviction should be quashed, *even at the risk of acquitting a guilty person*, or indeed an unknown number of guilty persons.[89]

The Commission was right to talk in terms of risk, but one may ask whether there are any missing words in the phrase 'if there is doubt about the safety of a conviction, the conviction should be quashed'. These words are tautological: the question of whether a conviction should be quashed is answered by deciding whether there is a doubt about safety; they amount to the same thing. More importantly, while the Commission was right to say that the appeal system should prioritise the acquittal of the innocent over the conviction of the guilty, how much should it prioritise the former over the latter? Should it prioritise the former to the complete exclusion of attempting to achieve the latter? If that was the case the Court would need to allow all appeals

88 J R Spencer, 'Criminal Law and Criminal Appeals: The Tail that Wags the Dog?' (1982) *Criminal Law Review* 260.

89 Law Commission, *Criminal Appeals: Consultation Paper* (Law Comm No 268, 2025) [4.114]. (Emphasis added).

against conviction because, as previously discussed, it is not possible to be certain that an appellant is guilty. Clearly, therefore, that is not a viable option. Instead, there is some degree of trade-off at the appeal stage, just as there was at the trial stage, between attempting to remedy the conviction of the innocent while at the same time upholding the convictions of the properly convicted.

The Court of Appeal is a creature of statute and is bound by the will of Parliament. Parliament has provided the unsafety test as the trigger for the Court to step in. Parliament has permitted / required the Court take the riskier path of upholding a conviction whenever it is satisfied that the conviction is safe. The Act does not specify what unsafety means, and, as discussed in Chapter 1, the provenance of the word 'safety' in the context of criminal appeals is rather vague. The Court has provided a detailed jurisprudence as to the situations in which a conviction will be unsafe, and there is a clear procedure to be followed in the different kinds of appeals that appear before it.[90] However, the unsafety test itself does not provide any baseline level of protection the Court should provide. Absent such a baseline it cannot be properly assessed how well the Court is performing or whether it should be providing more protection.[91] Furthermore, absent any baseline, it is not possible for the Court to achieve the minimal level of protection required; it will always face the accusation of being unduly cautious.

It is submitted that utilising the concept of risk helps to provide that baseline. The Court of Appeal does not talk in terms of risk or risk assessment, but it does talk in terms of safety and unsafety. Since something is safe when there is freedom from unacceptable risk, the question for the Court is whether the appellant has been protected from unacceptable risk. Whether an appellant has been protected depends upon whether the risk of wrongful conviction is ALARP. Consequently, appellants cannot expect to be protected from all risk; they can only expect that the risk is kept ALARP. This is essentially the same kind of risk that is taken during the trial; if the prosecution can produce a version of events that is more plausible than the defence's version, the risk that that version is mistaken is tolerated. This does create the risk that the Court's decision is wrong, and the Court would uphold the conviction of the innocent. While this is unwanted, as Poole J said in his remarks on risk (discussed earlier), that does not mean that the Court made the wrong decision based on all the information that was available at the time. When there are only two competing options available, it must choose the option which reduces the risk of injustice so that it is ALARP; it cannot be expected that it goes any further than that.

Risk in ordinary life is assessed by considering the severity of harm and the likelihood of that harm occurring. That provides a measure of risk, and

90 See Chapter 1.
91 As discussed in Chapter 1.

if the risk is ALARP there is freedom from unacceptable risk so the event in question is safe. It is not suggested that the Court of Appeal in any sense conducts such a risk assessment in its judgments. However, the assessment of risk can be applied to the unsafety test as a useful theoretical framework. Using this framework, dismissing an appeal against conviction engages a higher level of risk than allowing an appeal. This is because, in light of the problem of uncertainty, dismissing an appeal risks upholding the conviction of the innocent. Such a breach of the overriding objective would arguably constitute at least a very serious level of harm in qualitative risk assessment terms.

Where there is potential for a very serious level of harm, the risk engaged ranges from medium to very high depending upon how likely it is thought that that unwanted outcome will occur. Where an unwanted outcome with a very high severity of harm is thought to be very likely or almost certain to occur, the risk is either high or very high. That risk is far higher than tolerable and must not be allowed to materialise. The HSE said that any risk falling into the unacceptable region of its TOR framework must be ruled out unless it can be modified to reduce the risk or there are exceptional reasons.[92] In the context of criminal appeals, if the Court thinks that it is very likely an appellant is innocent, dismissing the appeal would be a high-risk activity and should not be done. Such a conviction must be unsafe because upholding the conviction would not protect the appellant from unacceptable risk.

However, in ordinary risk assessment terms, if the high-harm activity is thought very unlikely or unlikely, it might be said: implausible, the risk is reduced to medium, which can be tolerable so long as that risk is ALARP and the activity in question is worth the risk. Thus, when the Court is satisfied that it is unlikely the appellant is innocent, or the appellant has provided no plausible account that is inconsistent with his guilt, it is safe for the Court to dismiss the appeal if, but only if, it properly considers all the circumstances of the case and concludes that the wider (earlier) criminal proceedings have done everything it could do to keep the risk of injustice (all things considered, within the terms of the overriding objective) ALARP. In these circumstances the conviction is safe, because the appellant has been protected from unacceptable risk. As has been discussed, there is a possibility that this could lead to upholding the conviction of the innocent. As long as that risk has been properly assessed, the Court has discharged its obligation as it does not need to protect an appellant from all risk.

The other risk that is engaged in appeals against conviction is that it will quash the convictions of the guilty. Prima facie, quashing the convictions of the guilty is a serious level of harm, similar to upholding the convictions of the innocent. But it is somewhat more complicated. The Court cannot know whether the appellant is guilty, but if the Court thinks that the conviction should be

92 HSE (n 77) 42.

quashed because it is 'vitiated' by unfairness or other procedural irregularity, or by fresh evidence, there is a low risk of doing injustice because quashing the conviction in such circumstances itself represents the doing of justice. The severity of the harm caused would therefore be minor or trivial, because the doing of justice is the Court's overriding objective. Quashing the conviction should be done in such circumstances because there is a low or very low level of risk. Since the harm is minor and the likelihood of unwanted outcome is low, it follows that quashing the conviction would protect the appellant from unacceptable risk.

Where the Court finds that nothing went wrong at trial, which, as discussed in Chapter 1, occurs quite often, the key question for the Court is whether the risk of injustice is ALARP in circumstances where what is known about the case has not changed from what it was before the jury. If the Court is satisfied, given the weight of the evidence and everything that is known about the case by the time of the appeal, that there is a low likelihood the jury were wrong to be sure of guilt, then the risk has been properly assessed and the conviction can be safe. To be able to ascertain whether the appellant was protected from unacceptable risk by the trial process and the earlier parts of the process, the Court should consider the relative plausibility of the prosecution and the defence cases offered at trial. If it can sensibly be said that the prosecution case was not plausible with the appellant's innocence, then the Court is properly considering the veracity of the jury's verdict, and adequately protects the appellant from unacceptable risk.

By setting out the unsafety test as being a model of risk, it can be seen how the two aspects of severity x likelihood combine to provide a baseline as to when a conviction should be unsafe and provides the base line and the ceiling of the Court's powers. The Court can be expected to protect the appellant from unacceptable risk, not all risk. Consequently, the Court cannot be expected to incur costs in order to protect appellants so that the risk of injustice is lower than reasonably practicable. This serves to explain why the Court cannot be expected to allow all appeals against conviction; that would protect appellants from all risk, not merely unacceptable risk, but doing so would come at unreasonable cost. This also explains why the Court cannot treat all appeals against conviction as *de novo* review. As Nobles and Schiff said, doing so would impose the risk of expressing doubt upon the ability of the jury, as an institution, to reach correct conclusions.[93] Doing so would be an unreasonable step for the Court to take, or to expect the Court to take; it would have the benefit of protecting the appellant from additional risk, but would at significant cost, namely the undermining of the jury system.

93 R Nobles, D Schiff, 'The Supervision of Guilty Pleas by the Court of Appeal of England and Wales – Workable Relationships and Tragic Choices' (2020) *Criminal Law Forum* 513, 517.

The Court's decision-making in fresh evidence appeals, as noted, is more contentious. The supposition is that the Court is too cautious to allow appeals when the jury *could* have or *might* have acquitted on the basis of fresh evidence.[94] The problem with this supposition, it is argued, is that any fresh evidence, even if it is thought to be entirely unbelievable or discredited by the Court, *could* have led the jury to acquit. As Hughes LJ said in *Ahmed*: 'it will be impossible to be 100% sure that it might not possibly have had *some* impact on the jury's deliberations, since *ex hypoethesi* the jury has not seen the fresh material'.[95] As such, he said, that cannot be the test; the test must be whether the Court itself has a doubt.[96] It is submitted that Hughes must be right about that. The suggestion that the Court should consider whether the evidence *could* have had an impact would be, it is argued, an unreasonable step to take that would be seeking to reduce the risk of injustice more than in reasonably practicable. The Court cannot do that as that is not how risks are assessed. Subsequently, the Court's approach to fresh evidence cannot be realistically criticised.

Conclusion

Appeals against conviction take place in uncertain conditions, in which it can never be certain whether the appellant is guilty. This means there is always a risk of innocence. It has been argued that the unsafety test requires the Court to assess the risks that are involved in its available options, because something can only be 'safe' if there is freedom from unacceptable risk. All appellants appearing before the Court of Appeal are convicted; some of whom will have pleaded guilty, but the majority of which were convicted by a jury following an adversarial trial. Juries should only convict if they were sure. That does not require the jury to be certain; for that would be impossible. It has been argued, therefore, that the jury being sure represents the level of risk that is acceptable to the criminal justice system; if a jury was satisfied of guilt the criminal process is prepared to take the risk that the jury were wrong and proceed to punishment.

The Court of Appeal exists to provide a remedy in the inevitable but unknown cases that arise in which an injustice has been done, principally the conviction of the innocent. The Court of Appeal cannot know, better than any other part of the system, what the truth is. Accordingly, it needs to take a risk as well as assess the risks that have been accepted and ask whether those risks remain acceptable given everything that is now known about the case by the time of the conviction. So long as it is properly assessing those

94 See the Law Commission (n 89) [8.127].
95 [2010] EWCA Crim 2899 [24] (Emphasis original).
96 *Ahmed* (n 95) 24.

risks and considering the likelihood, based on the evidence, that the jury were wrong to be sure, the Court is protecting appellants from an unacceptable risk of wrongful conviction. It has been argued that this is what the Court does, and so its approach cannot be realistically criticised. This approach will be highlighted further in Chapter 3.

References

Allen, R J, Pardo, M S, 'Relative Plausibility and Its Critics' (2019) 23 *International Journal of Evidence and Proof* 5

Atkins, B T S, 'Building a Lexicon: The Contribution of Lexicography' (1991) 4 (3) *International Journal of Lexicography* 167

Bandle, T, 'Tolerability of Risk: The Regulator's Story' in Bouder, F, Salvin, D, Lofstedt, R E, (eds), *The Tolerability of Risk: A New Framework for Risk Management* (Earthscan, 2007)

Bar Standards Board, *Handbook* (BSB, 2026)

Bentham, J, *The Rationale of Punishment* (Robert Heward, 1830)

Biederman, A, Caruso, D, Kotsoglou, K N, 'Decision Theory, Relative Plausibility and the Criminal Standard of Proof' (2021) 15 *Criminal Law and Philosophy* 131

Boholm, M, Moller, N, Hansson, S O, 'The Concepts of Risk, Safety, and Security: Applications in Everyday Language' (2016) 36 (2) *Risk Analysis* 320

Boyle, T, *Health and Safety: Risk Management* (5th edn, Routledge, 2019)

Cohen, J, *An Introduction to the Philosophy of Induction and Probability* (Oxford University Press, 1989)

Commons Library, https://commonslibrary.parliament.uk/research-briefings/cbp-8372/

Concise Oxford English Dictionary (11th edn, Oxford University Press, 2008)

Crown Court Compendium

Crown Prosecution Service, *Code for Crown Prosecutors* (CPS, 2026)

Dennis, I, *The Law of Evidence* (8th edn, Oxford University Press, 2024)

Fenton, N, Lagnado, D, 'Bayesianism: Objections and Rebuttals' in Dahlman, C, Stein, A, Tuzet, G, (eds), *Philosophical Foundations of Evidence Law* (Oxford University Press, 2021)

Gillies, D, *Philosophical Theories of Probability* (Routledge, 2000)

Gross, S R, 'How Many False Convictions Are There? How Many Exonerations Are There?' in Huff, C R, Killias, M, (eds), *Wrongful Convictions and Miscarriages of Justice* (Routledge, 2013)

Gross, S R, O'Brien, B, 'Frequency and Predictors of False Conviction: Why We Know So Little, and New Data on Capital Cases' (2008) 5 (4) *Journal of Empirical Legal Studies* 927

Hájek, A, 'The Reference Class Problem Is Your Problem Too' (2007) 156 (3) *Synthese* 563

Hart, H L A, 'Prolegomenon to the Principles of Punishment' in Hart, H L A, (ed), *Punishment and Responsibility* (2nd edn, Oxford University Press, 2008)

Hastie, R, Dawes, R M, *Rational Choice in an Uncertain World* (Sage, 2001)

Health and Safety at Work etc Act 1974

Heffer, C N, 'The Language of Conviction and the Convictions of Certainty: Is "Sure" an Impossible Standard of Proof?' (2007) 5 (1) *International Commentary on Evidence* i

Hillier, T, Dingwall, G, *Criminal Justice and the Pursuit of Truth* (Bristol University Press, 2021)

HSE, *Reducing Risks, Protecting People: HSE Decision-Making Process* (HSE, 2001)

Human Rights Act 1998

Intelligence and Security Committee, *Report on the Intelligence Relating to the Murder of Fusilier Lee Rigby* (HC 795, 2014)

Kates, R W, Hohenemser, C, Kasperson, J, *Perilous Progress: Managing the Hazards of Technology* (Westview Press, 1985)

Keane, A, 'Not So Sure About the Criminal Standard of Proof' (2020) 170 (7898) *New Law Journal* 15

Law Commission, *Criminal Appeals: Consultation Paper* (Law Comm No 268, 2025)

Lindley, D V, *Understanding Uncertainty, Revised Edition* (John Wiley & Sons, 2014)

McKay, C, 'Predicting Risk in Criminal Procedure: Actuarial Tools, Algorithms, AI, and Judicial Decision-Making' (2020) 32 (1) *Current Issues in Criminal Justice* 22

McKeown, P, 'The Crown Court Compendium and the Criminal Standard of Proof: Suggestions to Aid Juror Comprehension and Help Judges' (2022) 11 *Criminal Law Review* 893

McKeown, P, Keane, A, Stares, S, 'Comprehension of "Sure" as the Description of the Criminal Standard of Proof: An Empirical Study' (2025) 9 *Criminal Law Review* 518

McQuaid, J, 'Historical Perspectives on the Tolerability of Risk' in Bouder, F, Salvin, D, Lofstedt, R E, (eds), *The Tolerability of Risk: A New Framework for Risk Management* (Earthscan, 2007)

Miller v Minister of Pensions [1947] 2 All ER 372

Ministry of Justice, https://www.gov.uk/government/statistics/criminal-justice-statistics-quarterly-september-2025

Ministry of Justice, *Root and Branch Review of the Parole System* (CP 654 2022)

Murphy-Oikonen, J, McQueen, K, Miller, A, Chambers, L, 'Gatekeepers to Justice: Police Officers' Experiences Responding to Sexual Assault' (2024) 70 (12) *Crime and Delinquency* 3442

Nicholson, D, 'Taking Epistemology Seriously: "Truth, Reason and Justice" Revisited' (2013) 17 (1) *International Journal of Evidence and Proof* 1

Nobles, R, Schiff, D, 'The Supervision of Guilty Pleas by the Court of Appeal of England and Wales – Workable Relationships and Tragic Choices' (2020) *Criminal Law Forum* 513

Oberdiek, J, *Imposing Risk: A Normative Framework* (Oxford University Press, 2017)

Oltedal, H A, 'Setting the Scene for Maritime Safety Management' in Oltedal, H A, Lützhöft, M, (eds), *Managing Maritime Safety* (Routledge, 2018)

Parole Board, *Types of Case Member Guidance* (Parole Board, 2023), https://www.gov.uk/government/publications/parole-board-types-of-cases-guidance-2023

Placani, A, Broadhead, S, 'Risk, Responsibility, and Their Relations' in Placani, A, Broadhead, S, (eds), *Risk and Responsibility in Context* (Routledge, 2024)
Police and Criminal Evidence Act 1984
R (on the application of DSD) v Parole Board for England and Wales [2019] QB 285
R v Adebolajo; Adebowale [2014] EWCA Crim 2779
R v Ahmed [2010] EWCA Crim 2899
R v Horseferry Road Magistrates ex parte Bennett [1994] 1 AC 42
Rawls, J, *A Theory of Justice Revised Edition* (Harvard University Press, 1999)
Re RS (Best Interests: Surgery and Intensive Care) [2025] EWCOP 38
Renn, O, 'The Risk Handling Chain' in Bouder, F, Salvin, D, Lofstedt, R E, (eds), *The Tolerability of Risk: A New Framework for Risk Management* (Earthscan, 2007)
Roberts, P, Zuckerman, A, *Roberts and Zuckerman's Criminal Evidence* (3rd edn, Oxford University Press, 2022)
Spencer, J R, 'Criminal Law and Criminal Appeals: The Tail that Wags the Dog?' (1982) *Criminal Law Review* 260
Spencer, J R, 'Quashing Convictions for Procedural Irregularities' (2007) *Criminal Law Review* 835
Stein, A, *Foundations of Evidence Law* (Oxford University Press, 2005)
Tadros, V, *The Ends of Harm: The Moral Foundations of Criminal Law* (Oxford University Press, 2011)
Trimpop, T M, *The Psychology of Risk Taking Behaviour* (Elsevier, 1994)
Twining, W, *Rethinking Evidence: Exploratory Essays* (2nd edn, Cambridge University Press, 2006)
Twining, W, 'Some Scepticism about Some Scepticisms' (1984) 11 *Journal of Law and Society* 137
UK Government, https://www.gov.uk/government/organisations/parole-board
UK Government, https://www.gov.uk/government/statistics/reported-road-casualties-great-britain-annual-report-2024/reported-road-casualties-great-britain-annual-report-2024#overall-casualties-and-rates
Walker, C, 'Miscarriages of Justice in Principle and Practice' in Walker, C, Starmer, K, (eds), *Miscarriages of Justice: A Review of Justice in Error* (Oxford University Press, 1999)
Yates, J F, Stone, E R, 'The Risk Construct' in Yates, J F, (ed), *Risk-Taking Behaviour* (John Wiley and Sons, 1992)
Zander, M, 'The Criminal Standard of Proof: How Sure Is Sure?' (2000) 150 (1517) *New Law Journal* 18

3 A year in the Court of Appeal (Criminal Division)

Taking risks January–December 2024

Introduction

The Court does not talk in terms of risk in its judgments, but it does talk in terms of safety and unsafety. Since something is safe only when there is freedom from unacceptable risk, the unsafety test maps onto the assessment of risk. This chapter presents the results of a qualitative study of judgments handed down in the calendar year 2024. Utilising risk assessment as a theoretical framework for analysis, the purpose of this study is to scrutinise the Court's assessment of risk. It will be shown that the Court does assess risk, and accordingly the risk assessment lens is a suitable one through which to scrutinise the Court's decisions. It is ultimately concluded that the Court does generally adequately protect appellants from unacceptable risk, but there are some areas in which the Court could be more protective.

The risk assessment lens

The core premise of this book is that the function of the Court of Appeal is to protect appellants from the unacceptable risk of injustice; it does not need to protect them from all risk. The Court of Appeal does not talk in terms of risk or risk assessment; it talks in terms of safety and unsafety. Most likely, the Court would not think it is taking a risk, because it is 'sure' the conviction is safe / unsafe. However, as discussed in Chapter 2, the concept of risk maps closely onto the concept of unsafety in the context of criminal appeals. To establish that the Court is assessing the risk appropriately, one should see in judgments the Court assessing the likelihood of wrongful conviction and checking that the risk was kept as low as reasonably practicable. In particular, it should be assessing whether the appellant version of events is more plausible than the prosecution's so there can be no reasonable doubt about guilt. This will help it to decide whether its own decision to dismiss an appeal protects the appellant from unacceptable risk.

DOI: 10.4324/9781003782292-4

There have been many studies of the Court of Appeal involving quantitative analysis of its judgments.[1] Most often these studies produce figures and statistics relating to the decision-making of the Court. As a result of such studies, it is well established what kinds of issues tend to be raised in appeals, how likely certain kinds of grounds of appeal are to be successful, and so on. Consequently, there is little to be gained by a further quantitative study of the Court covering the same ground. The focus of this chapter is the Court's routine decision-making between 01 January 2024 and 31 December 2024. The objective is to provide an empirical snapshot of the Court's decision-making in one calendar year through the lens of risk.

The focus is on the Court's *routine* decision-making rather than high-profile, contentious, or particularly important cases. Most appeals against conviction disappear into the history of the Court, never to be seen or heard from again. Most appeals are rather simple questions of whether an alleged error occurred at trial and the potential impact of any error if one did occur. Few appeals have any precedential value to later appeals and turn purely on the assessment of facts. This is not the impression that one might obtain from reading law reports or popular or academic press discussion of the Court's decision-making. Such reports are obviously skewed towards the more legally complex, important, noteworthy, or problematic cases. This skewness might provide an inaccurate picture of the Court's decision-making and may present the Court's approach as being more problematic than it actually is (because it is these appeals that are reported upon and debated). Thus, by focussing in a systematic manner upon the Court's routine decision-making on appeals that otherwise may well have gone unreported and largely unknown, the chapter presents a more accurate representation of the Court's tolerance for risk.

A list of appeals against conviction and renewed applications for permission to appeal handed down between 01 January 2024 and 31 December 2024 was downloaded from the *Westlaw, Lexis UK,* and *National Archives* websites. The result was a dataset of 101 appeals against conviction (39 of which were allowed, and 62 of which were dismissed), and 195 renewed applications for permission to appeal (three of which were granted permission). The total

1 Eg M Knight, *Criminal Appeals* (Stephen and Sons, 1970); K Malleson, *The Royal Commission on Criminal Justice Research Study No 17* (HMSO, 1993); S Roberts, 'Fresh Evidence and Factual Innocence in the Criminal Division of the Court of Appeal' (2017) 81 (4) *Journal of Criminal Law* 303; P Dargue, 'The Safety of Convictions in the Court of Appeal: Fresh Evidence in the Criminal Division through an Empirical Lens' (2019) 83 (6) *Journal of Criminal Law* 433; P Dargue, 'An Analysis of Disclosure Failings in Murder Appeals Against Conviction' (2020) *Criminal Law Review* 707; P Dargue, 'The Tolerability of Risk in the Court of Appeal (Criminal Division): An Empirical Study of Appeals against Conviction' (2025) 12 *Criminal Law Review* 743; B Brewis, P Dargue, 'Sexual Behaviour Evidence in the Court of Appeal (Criminal Division): Presenting the Need for Reform' (2025) 89 (6) *Journal of Criminal Law* 279.

sample is, therefore, 296 cases. These figures do not tally with the Court's official reports,[2] and so it must be the case that this is not the full universe of appeals or renewed applications decided by the Court in that year. This is not problematic for the discussion to follow because there is no intention that the findings be generalised to appeals outside of the sample; it should therefore be understood as a discussion of the appeals in this sample only. For the reasons noted here, there is little further statistical or quantitative analysis of the these cases. The main focus of analysis will be the 101 full appeals, because it is only those which apply the unsafety test.[3] However, renewed applications will be discussed where appropriate to illustrate the Court's assessment of risk and question whether its risk toleration is appropriate.

Criminal Appeals 2024

Procedural irregularity appeals

As discussed in Chapter 1, the first stage in procedural irregularity appeals is to determine whether the alleged error occurred. There are typically three outcomes that follow from this initial decision: 1) the Court finds no irregularity occurred and dismisses the appeal, 2) the Court finds that an irregularity occurred and allows the appeal, 3) the Court finds an irregularity did occur and it dismisses the appeal.

In this sample, where the Court found that an irregularity had occurred, it would consistently apply the *Davis* test of whether, had the irregularity not occurred, the only reasonable and proper verdict would have been one of guilty.[4] To that end, the Court's approach is clear, consistent, and in line with the unsafety test. There was ample evidence of the Court being willing to reverse jury verdicts when there was good reason to do so. In the language of risk, it can be said that in such cases the Court was required to act to protect the appellant from unacceptable risk. For instance, in *LMS*[5] the appellant complained that the trial judge's summing up contained inaccuracies and was unbalanced in favour of the prosecution. In quashing the conviction, the Court said that the trial judge had strayed across the line, giving rise to an imbalance.[6] The credibility of the complainant was central, and the judge's directions as to how to approach the evidence had the effect of shoring-up the prosecution's case.[7] The conviction was quashed because the irregularity went to the root of the jury's task.

2 See Court of Appeal, *Annual Report 2023–2024*, Annex D.
3 Renewed applications apply ask whether the grounds are reasonably arguable.
4 *R v Davis, Rowe, and Johnson* [2001] 1 Cr App R 8.
5 *R v LMS* [2024] EWCA Crim 96.
6 *R v LMS* [2024] EWCA Crim 35.
7 *R v LMS* [2024] EWCA Crim 42.

In *Smith*[8] the appeal was allowed because the Court thought that a misdirection by the trial judge 'may have held some real significance to the jury's discussions and conclusions'.[9] In *McNaughten*[10] the convictions were quashed because it thought the judge's summing up indicated partiality towards the prosecution.[11] In *Head*[12] the trial judge had incorrectly admitted (what was proffered to be) bad character evidence, and subsequently misdirected the jury as to how to use it.[13] In allowing the appeal the Court said that 'the jury were left with a substantial body of evidence which had no relevance to the issue of whether a sexual assault had occurred. Despite that, they were told that it might have some relevance to that issue'.[14]

It is worth nothing that in none of these cases was the appellant proved innocent, yet the convictions were quashed. In risk terms employed in this book, the Court of Appeal did protect these appellants from unacceptable risk because it quashed the convictions. But it should not be assumed that, despite quashing these convictions, the Court is prepared to, or should, protect appellants from all risk when an irregularity did occur at trial. The key question is whether the irregularity in question vitiated the conviction on procedural grounds, or whether the irregularity went to a core aspect of the case and the jury's task. This is the dividing line that the Court has drawn between what is an acceptable and unacceptable risk. In the aforementioned cases the convictions did cross over that line; upholding the convictions would have meant that the Court was not protecting the appellants from unacceptable risk. But it is, in general, not easy for an appellant to demonstrate that dismissing appeal would place him at unacceptable risk.

Amongst the sample full appeals against conviction (i.e. not the renewed applications), the Court found in 53 cases (52%) that no irregularity had occurred, and all such appeals were dismissed. Almost all the renewed applications for permission to appeal found that no irregularity had occurred. As discussed in Chapter 1, these appeals are essentially converted into 'lurking doubt' appeals once the Court finds that no irregularity occurred because the Court must still consider the question of unsafety. If there is a reasonable doubt about guilt then the conviction cannot be upheld, for that would obviously place the appellant at unacceptable risk. One of the criticisms made towards the Court is that it is unduly deferential towards the jury's verdict, especially when it finds nothing had gone wrong at trial.[15] This leads to the question of

8 *R v Ben Smith* [2024] EWCA Crim 342.
9 *Smith* (n 8) 50.
10 *R v McNaughton* [2024] EWCA Crim 1129.
11 *R v McNaughton* [2024] EWCA Crim 15.
12 *R v Head* [2024] EWCA Crim 1487.
13 *R v Head* [2024] EWCA Crim 33–36.
14 *R v Head* [2024] EWCA Crim 36.
15 See Malleson; Roberts (n 1).

whether the Court is too tolerant of the risk in appeals such as these where it finds that no irregularity occurred.

Reading the appeals decided in 2024, however, leads to the conclusion that there is an element of unreality in the view that the Court is in some general sense too deferential towards the jury. In truth, it is submitted, a large number of appeals were optimistic and the Court's tolerance of risk cannot be reasonably disputed; the appellant's case was not plausible. Attention now turns to consider some of these appeals in more depth.

General observations – optimistic appeals

Most appeals, it is suggested, were easily and convincingly dispensed with by the Court. As such, while any appellant could in fact be innocent, there is no reason to think that the Court was unduly tolerant of the risk of injustice. One example is *Menzies and others.*[16] The appellant had been convicted of murder after stabbing the victim in a robbery. His appeal against conviction was based on the supposition that the trial judge made several errors that amounted to procedural irregularities in his summing up to the jury.[17] The problem with that submission, the Court said, was that (even if the supposition was true, which the Court did not accept) the judge had accurately directed the jury elsewhere about intention, including in the written route to verdict and on at least five other occasions.[18] The appeal was dismissed.

In *BVY,*[19] the appellant had been convicted of sexual offences and appealed on the basis that the trial judge was wrong to refuse to admit non-defendant bad character (relating to one of the complainants). The alleged bad character evidence related to a single note in the complainant's school record which, the appellant said, undermined her credibility.[20] The trial judge said that the evidence fell 'far short' of being of substantial probative value and concluded that the judge's decision was not *Wednesbury* unreasonable.[21] The Court said, convincingly, that there was no merit in the challenge to the judge's ruling and no basis for treating any of the convictions as unsafe.[22] In risk terms, reading the judgment one sees the Court properly assessing the trial process against the weight of the evidence. The appellant could be innocent, but it cannot be said he offered a plausible alternative to the prosecution (which, in any event, was rejected by the jury) and that there was unacceptable risk.

16 *R v Menzies* [2024] EWCA Crim 1549.
17 *R v Menzies* [2024] EWCA Crim 27–28.
18 *R v Menzies* [2024] EWCA Crim 35.
19 *R v BVY* [2024] EWCA Crim 1355.
20 *R v BVY* [2024] EWCA Crim 15–18.
21 *R v BVY* [2024] EWCA Crim 44.
22 *R v BVY* [2024] EWCA Crim 46.

In *Jodeiri-Lakpour*[23] the issue was whether the judge was wrong not to give a recent complaint direction to the jury.[24] The Court doubted that it was necessary on the facts, or that it was a material error.[25] The Court was clear that failure to give such a direction does not automatically render the conviction unsafe; instead, 'attention must be directed to the relevance of the missing direction'.[26] The appeal was dismissed, the Court being of the view that the jury understood their task and so it was satisfied the conviction was safe. Once again, this was an appeal easily and convincingly dispensed with. *Ali*[27] concerned the question of whether the trial judge was wrong to admit a hearsay statement and / or whether it should have been excluded by the trial judge's general power to exclude prosecution evidence under section 78 of PACE. The Court held that the way in which the evidence reached the jury was not entirely satisfactory,[28] but that the conviction was safe due to the overwhelming evidence and that the appellant's case depended on a number of 'wholly implausible coincidences'.[29] It has to be said that it is not possible to challenge that conclusion, and the Court was properly assessing the weight of the evidence.

The cases of *Hill*,[30] *Wilson; Smith*,[31] *Galbraith*,[32] and *BJK*[33] all concerned appellants who argued that the trial judge was wrong to exclude evidence under section 41 of the Youth Justice and Criminal Evidence Act 1999. In all cases the Court held that trial judge was correct, that there was nothing to doubt the safety of the conviction, and that the convictions were safe. Section 41 places strict limits on the admissibility into evidence of a sexual offence complainant's sexual behaviour. It is true that these appellants could have been innocent. But from a risk perspective, it is the law that the admission of sexual behaviour evidence is tightly controlled. The Court said in *Hill* that if the appellant's (proffered) evidence was admissible 'it would undermine the whole purpose of s.41 which is to limit a complainant's exposure to being cross-examined'.[34] In *Galbraith* the Court said that section 41 was enacted in pursuit of 'a legitimate objective to protect complainants from . . . indignity and humiliating questioning'.[35] It is submitted that the Court's assessment of risk cannot be faulted.

23 *R v Jodeiri-Lakpour* [2024] EWCA Crim 97.
24 *R v Jodeiri-Lakpour* [2024] EWCA Crim 21.
25 *R v Jodeiri-Lakpour* [2024] EWCA Crim 26 and 39.
26 *R v Jodeiri-Lakpour* [2024] EWCA Crim 30.
27 *R v Ali* [2024] EWCA Crim 77.
28 *R v Ali* [2024] EWCA Crim 45.
29 *R v Ali* [2024] EWCA Crim 47.
30 *R v Hill* [2024] EWCA Crim 1423.
31 *R v Wilson* [2024] EWCA Crim 1514.
32 *R v Galbraith* [2024] EWCA Crim 1148.
33 *R v BJK* [2024] EWCA Crim 667.
34 *Hill* (n 30) 47.
35 *Galbraith* (n 32) 23.

The aforementioned cases (which are only selective cases evidencing the Court's acceptable approach towards risk), it is submitted, demonstrate that most appeals had limited realistic prospect of success. If anything, rather than the Court being too cautious, it might suggest that the permission stage was too generous in granting permission. Certainly, the Court would regularly state, even in appeals that had received permission, that there was no merit to the appeal.[36] In truth, most appellants do not come close to showing they were even at any plausible risk of injustice. It is true that all these appellants could in fact have been innocent. But, having been convicted by the jury, they need to adduce some plausible claim if they are to convince the Court that the conviction is unsafe. The majority of appellants in this sample were not able to come close to doing so. In the absence of some cogent reason for having any doubt about safety, the Court would need to do more than reasonably practicable to protect these appellants from injustice: allow an appeal in the absence of any doubt. The general impression gained from reading these appeals is that it cannot be said the Court was too tolerant of the risk of injustice.

The chapter now turns to particular grounds and how risk was assessed.

Inconsistent verdicts

In *Mundle*[37] the appellant argued that conviction for one count of rape was inconsistent with his being acquitted of a further count of rape arising from the same circumstances. The argument was easily, and convincingly, dispensed with by the Court which observed that the jury not being sure that the ingredients of the second offence had been made out did not require them to treat the complainant as unreliable on the first count.[38] In *Kent*[39] the appellant argued that his acquittal for the offence of having an offensive weapon (a baseball bat) was inconsistent with his conviction for wounding (striking the complainant with the same baseball bat). The suggestion was rejected by the Court. In *BAA*[40] the appellant was convicted of one count on an eight-count indictment alleging indecent assault; the jury was unable to agree on the remaining counts. He argued that the conviction was inconsistent with the others. The Court's response was that there was evidence which would entitle the jury to convict and so was not inconsistent with the other counts for which no verdict was returned.[41]

36 See eg *R v BVY* [2024] EWCA Crim 1355 [46]; *R v Hanna* [2024] EWCA Crim 1315 [100]; *R v Serdoud* [2024] EWCA Crim 1398 [30]; *R v BJS* [2024] EWCA Crim 1356 [47].
37 *R v Mundle* [2024] EWCA Crim 1289.
38 *R v Mundle* [2024] EWCA Crim 37.
39 *R v Kent* [2024] EWCA Crim 1271.
40 *R v BAA* [2024] EWCA Crim 343.
41 *R v BAA* [2024] EWCA Crim 35.

Appeals based on inconsistent verdicts are particularly difficult for appellants; no appellants in this sample were able to argue successfully that their convictions were inconsistent with any other verdicts following trial. In the terms of risk used in this book it is easy to see why. It is difficult to see how upholding a conviction for no other reason than it is (allegedly) inconsistent with other verdicts (typically with acquittals) would generally place appellants at unacceptable risk. If the appellant has been acquitted on some counts but convicted on others he has already done better than he might have done. It also, arguably, evidences a thoughtful and sensitive jury who must have considered the counts separately as they would have been directed to do by the trial judge. It is difficult to convince the Court, and quite unpalatable for the Court to accept, that the jury's decision-making approach was flawed on the counts that went against the appellant but acceptable on those that went in his favour. There is a danger that the Court will think that it was the acquittal that was generous (and inconsistent) with the conviction.[42] On the face of it, therefore, there is no obvious reason why the Court should not have been prepared to tolerate the residual risk that was involved in dismissing these appeals.

No case to answer

Appeals concerning rulings on submission of 'no case to answer' are particularly pertinent because the Court needs to assess the weight of the evidence to determine whether the trial judge was wrong to reject an application of no case to answer. The appellant in *Heaven*[43] had been convicted of intimidating a witness. The allegation was that the complainant, who had assisted the police in an investigation about the appellant having assaulted another person, was assaulted and called 'a snitch' by him. A submission of no case to answer was made on the basis that there was no evidence Heaven had assaulted the complainant in the knowledge that she had previously assisted the police. The trial judge rejected the submission, but the Court of Appeal said it should have succeeded. The prosecution evidence, 'taken at its highest, was not capable of making a jury sure of the appellant's knowledge or suspicion that [the complainant] had assisted the police'.[44] This could hardly be considered a cautious or 'narrow' decision; if anything it appeared rather generous. It shows the Court taking a robust approach to the assessment of whether the trial process adequately protected the appellant from unacceptable risk.

In *Smith and others*,[45] several convictions were quashed because the trial judge should have removed some counts due to there being no case to answer.

42 See *Kent* (n 39) at [59] which evidenced this line of reasoning.
43 *R v Heaven* [2024] EWCA Crim 88.
44 *R v Heaven* [2024] EWCA Crim 14.
45 *R v Mark Smith* [2024] EWCA Crim 390.

These counts were the only allegations in which a date, time, and place were specifically alleged in the indictment, but it had been proven that the abuse could not have occurred at that time in the manner alleged.[46] On the face of it, the appellants were innocent of those counts as specifically described on the indictment and were victims of a miscarriage of justice in relation to those counts. The Court said that the trial judge had 'strained to find a route by which to explain "these obvious weaknesses" of the evidence'.[47] In relation to these specific counts only, the Court did not think a reasonable jury properly directed 'could on the evidence, reject all realistic possibilities consistent with innocence'.[48] Again, the Court was robustly defending the right of an appellant to be protected from unacceptable risk.

Determining whether there was a case to answer is a delicate matter. If the Court finds there was no case to answer the appeal must be allowed, and so it is not a decision taken lightly. In *Banner; Bennett*[49] two appellants had been convicted of various counts of ill-treatment of a person in care. The question for the trial judge was whether the appellants' actions (which concerned, in part, 'twanging' balloons at the complainant knowing she did not like balloons) could amount to 'ill-treatment'. The appellants made a submission of no case to answer, asserting the behaviour could not amount to ill-treatment, but the judge rejected the submission and the trial proceeded. The appellants appealed challenging the judge's interpretation of the Act and saying the judge should have acceded to the submission of no case to answer. The Court of Appeal held that there was a case to answer so dismissed the appeal. The case received some academic treatment with no suggestions that the Court's decision was even arguably wrong.[50] The fact is that the appellant's conviction depended squarely upon the assessment of the jury, and there was ample evidence of the appellant's acts (including covert recording by an undercover BBC *Panorama* journalist). It is impossible to say there was an unacceptable risk of injustice.

Another no case to answer appeal was *Smith and others*.[51] The appellants, 'Just Stop Oil' protesters, had entered the racetrack at Silverstone during the British Grand Prix. They were subsequently variously convicted of causing and/or conspiracy to cause a public nuisance contrary to section 78 of the Police, Crime, Sentencing, and Courts Act 2022. Several of the appellants had made a submission of no case to answer at trial, arguing that they had not created a risk of serious harm to a sector of the public within the terms of the 2022

46 *R v Mark Smith* [2024] EWCA Crim 41–44.
47 *R v Mark Smith* [2024] EWCA Crim 52.
48 *R v Mark Smith* [2024] EWCA Crim 51.
49 *R v Matthew Banner; R v Peter Bennett* [2024] EWCA Crim 1201.
50 See Anon, 'Ill-treatment of a Patient' 10 *Archbold Review* 3; P Hungerford-Welch, 'Ill-Treatment of a Person in Care' (2025) 2 *Criminal Law Review* 102.
51 *R v Joshua Smith* [2024] EWCA Crim 1040.

Act.[52] The Court agreed with the trial judge that, upon a correct interpretation of the Act, there was a case to answer and the appeal was dismissed. These appellants were the first persons convicted of an offence under the 2022 Act; that Act having abolished the common law relating to public nuisance.[53] It is therefore legally an important case which received academic treatment.[54] The question to be addressed is whether the Court's decision subjected the appellants to an unacceptable risk of injustice; it is submitted that it cannot be said the appellants were so subjected. Not least, this is because the appellants did not contest that they did the acts in question and so the only question was the Court of Appeal's interpretation of the relevant Act. While the Court could have interpreted the Act differently, its interpretation is not clearly wrong and so it is difficult to see how the appellants were subject to unacceptable risk.

Finally, in *F*[55] the appellant had been convicted of indecent assault. Defence counsel made a submission of no case to answer, asserting that there was no evidence of 'assault' in relation to the alleged indecent assault. The supposition was that there was no evidence that the appellant himself had moved, rather than remaining completely passive during the alleged act.[56] There was long-standing authority for the suggestion that in relation to that specific offence an 'assault' requires active force,[57] including a decision of the Court of Appeal as recently as 2015.[58] The Court, however, felt able to distinguish that line of authority on the basis that the previous authorities were concerned with touching of the defendant by the complainant and not with penetration by the defendant of the complainant.[59] The appeal was dismissed, the Court finding there was a case to answer, and rejecting a ground of appeal based on the summing up.

It has to be said that the Court's reasoning is suspect.[60] Chen criticised the decision not on the supposition that the appeal should have been allowed (quite the contrary), but on the ground that the Court should have dismissed the appeal by overturning or not following the earlier authorities rather than seeking to distinguish them.[61] It is important to remember that appeals are not academic exercises. The law relating to indecent assault was (and remains)

52 *R v Joshua Smith* [2024] EWCA Crim 13.
53 *R v Joshua Smith* [2024] EWCA Crim 42.
54 See (2024) 9 *Archbold Review* 2; N Parpworth, 'Public Nuisance and the Meaning of a "Section of the Public"' (2025) 89 (1) *Journal of Criminal Law* 52; A Benn, 'Causing a Public Nuisance' (2025) 1 *Criminal Law Review* 45.
55 *R v F* [2024] EWCA Crim 463.
56 *R v F* [2024] EWCA Crim 28.
57 Eg *Fairclough v Whipp* (1951) 35 Cr App R 138; *DPP v Rogers* (1953) 37 Cr App R 137.
58 *R v Dunn* [2015] EWCA Crim 724.
59 *F* (n 55) 57.
60 C Chen, 'A Missed Opportunity to Correct the Law on Indecent Assault against Children' (2025) 89 (6) *Journal of Criminal Law* 349.
61 C Chen, 'A Missed Opportunity to Correct the Law on Indecent Assault against Children' (2025) 89 (6) *Journal of Criminal Law* 352.

in an unsatisfactory state,[62] but the Court was faced with an appellant who, in counsel for the prosecution's words, was asserting a case which 'does not reflect physiological reality'[63] (i.e. the assertion that he was not an 'active participant' when committing an indecent assault against a child). It is not clear why the Court thought it was not the 'time or the place'[64] to resolve this difficulty in the law, given, at least in part, that is the role of the Court. Nevertheless, factually, there is no reason to doubt the accuracy of the conviction – the appellant did not call any evidence in his defence.[65] The appellant could have been innocent, but to quash the conviction, it is suggested, would have offered greater protection than he was entitled to: which is only freedom from unacceptable risk, not any risk at all.

Unfair trials

Appellants have a right to a fair trial by the Human Rights Act 1998. The relationship between fairness and unsafety is difficult, and there is arguably a small gap between the two, in which a trial being unfair does not automatically render a conviction unsafe.[66] In *Togher* the Court of Appeal said that where a trial has been unfair, it is 'almost inevitable' that the conviction must be unsafe.[67] However, this point is not altogether clear; 'almost inevitable' is not the same as inevitable. In *Dundon*[68] the Court said that whether a conviction is rendered unsafe will 'depend on the kind of breach and the nature and quality of the evidence in the case'.[69]

Appellants can, and do, assert that their convictions should be quashed because the trial was overall unfair. In the 2024 sample of renewed applications, assertions that the trial was unfair were made regularly but obtained little success. For example, in *Kutek,*[70] *Zulfiqar,*[71] *Ward,*[72] and *Khan,*[73] generalised allegations of unfairness were dispensed with by the Court simply asserting that nothing unfair had occurred. *N* obtained permission to appeal on ground 1 on the basis that

62 See C Sjolin, 'The Need to Kill off Zombie Law: Indecent Assault, Where It Went Wrong and How to Put It Right' (2017) 81 *Journal of Criminal Law* 50.
63 *F* (n 55) 30.
64 *F* (n 55) 56.
65 *F* (n 55) 12.
66 See N Taylor, D Ormerod, 'Mind the Gaps: Safety, Fairness, and Moral Legitimacy' (2004) *Criminal Law Review* 266.
67 *R v Togher* [2001] 3 All ER 463 [33].
68 *R v Dundon* [2004] EWCA Crim 621.
69 *R v Dundon* [2004] EWCA Crim 15.
70 *R v Kutek* [2024] EWCA Crim 1675.
71 *R v Zulfiqar and others* [2024] EWCA Crim 1710.
72 *R v Ward* [2024] EWCA Crim 1696.
73 *R v Khan* [2024] EWCA Crim 148.

interventions by the trial judge may have rendered the trial unfair.[74] The Court thought it arguable that his interventions during examination in chief may have crossed the line and the question of whether that rendered the conviction unsafe would need to be properly argued out.[75] It is clear that general assertions have little prospect of success of even being granted permission to appeal.

In relation to appeals that appeared before the Court in 2024, many appellants alleged that an irregularity meant there was some degree of unfair*ness* in their trial. A direct assertation that the trial was on the whole unfair was less common. Of those who could demonstrate the trial was unfair, the appeal was always allowed. The convictions in *Reid* were quashed because several of the judge's case management decisions meant he did not receive the fair trial he was entitled to.[76] In *Fisher* convictions for racially aggravated intentional harassment and assault by beating were quashed because the appellant did not receive a fair trial.[77] Fisher's trial eventually got underway after a number of delays. He did not appear for the first day of his trial and counsel informed the judge he was not contactable. The trial proceeded in his absence and he was convicted. Several days after conviction the appellant's solicitors learned that he had been in hospital under sedation for the duration of his trial. The Court quashed the convictions because 'whether or not the original decision was technically correct, its effect was that the applicant was denied the possibility of a fair trial for reasons which we now know are no fault of his'.[78]

The Court would scrutinise carefully the allegation that the trial was unfair. The case of *Brooker* provides one example.[79] The Court described the appellant's trial counsel's approach, in which he refused to cross-examine the complainant, as 'recalcitrant and unprincipled.'[80] It said there was a catalogue of professional errors, and that his performance fell below the standards expected of a member of the Bar.[81] Despite this, the Court said that the trial was not unfair. Any unfairness, the Court said, was to the prosecution and not the defence because it (the prosecution) did not have the defence case put to it.[82] It is submitted that in this case in particular, the Court stretched credibility by saying the trial was not unfair; if this trial was not unfair it is difficult to understand what would be unfair. It would seem, if this case is taken as a precedent, almost impossible for conduct of trial counsel to render a trial unfair. From a risk perspective this is problematic; while the Court

74 *R v N* [2024] EWCA Crim 489.
75 *R v N* [2024] EWCA Crim [48].
76 *R v Reid* [2024] EWCA Crim 308 [35].
77 *R v Fisher* [2024] EWCA Crim 1605.
78 *R v Fisher* [2024] EWCA Crim 10.
79 *R v Brooker* [2024] EWCA Crim 103.
80 *R v Brooker* [2024] EWCA Crim 102.
81 *R v Brooker* [2024] EWCA Crim 115–116.
82 *R v Brooker* [2024] EWCA Crim 118.

does not need to protect from all risk, it should not make the hurdle to be surmounted impossibly high.

Abuse of process and stays

Amongst the renewed applications, the applicant would often make generalised assertions that the trial was an abuse of process, allegations which were invariably dismissed by the Court.[83] In the (generally limited) information provided, it is impossible to say the Court was wrong to do so. The issue was given greater consideration in *Letby.*[84] Letby argued that adverse publicity surrounding her convictions meant that her later trial should have been stayed as an abuse of process. The Court said that the decision as to a stay was an exercise of judgment rather than discretion; as such, the question was whether the decision was wrong.[85] The Court noted that to stay a criminal trial is an exceptional remedy of last resort.[86] It can be deduced that finding the judge was in error will, therefore, be an onerous task. Whilst this is not a problem in principle, it is important that the Court does not raise the hurdle too high, or it may impose unacceptable risk.

One kind of appeal regularly raised abuse of process grounds: appeals relating to appellants / applicants asserting they committed crimes as a victim of trafficking (VOT). There is a defence to crime if the defendant can show they were a VOT in section 45 of the Modern Slavery Act 2015. Appellants in these cases would typically argue that they were improperly advised about the defence, and had they would not have pleaded guilty had they been properly advised. Typically, they would adduce fresh evidence of their status as a victim of trafficking. Where the appellant took the matter to trial, appellants would argue that if the trial judge had known of the defence and / or the appellant's status as a VOT, the trial would have been stayed or the prosecution would have withdrawn.

Most appellants in the sample who raised this issue had a positive Conclusive Grounds Decision (CGD) that he / she was a VOT issued by the Single Competent Authority (SCA, part of the Home Office).[87] The Court in *AAD* had earlier affirmed that the CGD is admissible as fresh evidence.[88] In *AAJ*[89] the Lady Chief Justice said that there is no blanket immunity for a VOT; there must be a reasonable nexus between the offence and the

83 See for example: *R v Brassard* [2024] EWCA Crim 1852; *R v Zulfiqar* [2024] EWCA Crim 1710;

84 *R v Letby* [2024] EWCA Crim 1278.

85 *R v Letby* [2024] EWCA Crim 11.

86 *R v Letby* [2024] EWCA Crim 26.

87 See *R v FGH* [2024] EWCA Crim 1353 at [16]; *R v BNN* [2024] EWCA Crim 991 [21].

88 *R v ADD and others* [2022] EWCA Crim 106.

89 *R v AJJ and others* [2021] EWCA Crim 1278.

trafficking.[90] Noting that the real question – the extent to which the offences were consequent upon the exploitation – is a 'truly fact-sensitive decision', her Ladyship observed that the CGD is not binding on the Court but it would normally respect it.[91]

While accepting that these are indeed highly fact specific decisions, in the 2024 appeals there is evidence of differing approaches and, it is suggested, questionable tolerance of risk. In some cases the Court was respectful of the CGD and empathetic of the appellant,[92] in other cases highly doubtful or even dismissive of the CGD.[93] In one case (*BNN*) the Court seemed to hold that evidence of fresh fruit and laundered clothes evidenced lack of compulsion despite a CGD.[94] In *TT* the renewed application for permission to appeal was refused because he knew about the section 45 defence, and explicitly said he had been trafficked in his defence statement, and had since received a CGD, but chose to plead guilty instead.[95] This appeared a particularly harsh decision which arguably did not provide adequate protection from the risk of injustice.

Fresh evidence

The Court's approach in fresh evidence appeals was discussed in some detail earlier in this book. There are two stages to a fresh evidence appeal: first, the question of whether the Court will receive the evidence, and secondly whether the evidence (if admitted) causes the conviction to be unsafe. The test for admitting fresh evidence is the 'interests of justice' test in section 23(1) of the 1968 Act. In deciding whether it is in the interests of justice to receive the evidence it is required to consider the factors in section 23(2), which for ease of reference are now reproduced:

(a) whether the evidence appears to be capable of belief
(b) whether the evidence may afford a ground for allowing the appeal
(c) whether the evidence would be admissible
(d) whether there is a reasonable explanation for failure to adduce the evidence at trial

The Law Commission was concerned that the Court would sometimes treat these factors as the criteria for admission, rather than mere factors.[96] It is argued that,

90 *R v AJJ and others* [2021] EWCA Crim 39.
91 *R v AJJ and others* [2021] EWCA Crim 39.
92 Eg. *R v AAB* [2024] EWCA Crim 880.
93 Eg. *R v FGH* [2024] EWCA Crim 1353; *R v BNN* [2024] EWCA Crim 991.
94 *BNN* (n 87) 69.
95 *R v TT* [2024] EWCA Crim 616.
96 Law Commission, *Criminal Appeals: Consultation Paper* (Law Comm No 268, 2025) [6.108].

on the basis of appeals that were handed down in 2024, the Court's approach to assessing the strength of fresh evidence cannot reasonably be said to place appellants at unacceptable risk. Similar to concerns regarding the Court's approach in procedural irregularity appeals, it is submitted that there is a sense of unreality about the claim that the Court is too narrow / too tolerant of risk in fresh evidence appeals once the Court's routine decision-making is included in the analysis. Most fresh evidence did not plausibly challenge the prosecution's case. However, that said, there are some identifiable problems with the Court's handling of fresh evidence which might, in places, put appellants at unacceptable risk.

Appeals allowed

There were 16 full appeals against conviction and 50 applicants who sought to adduce fresh evidence. Twelve of the 16 (75%) fresh evidence appeals were allowed. Three of these cases were appeals relating to the Post Office *Horizon* scandal.[97] Five of the fresh evidence appeals (three of which were allowed and two dismissed) were appeals relating to fresh evidence of trafficking, which was discussed previously. There was one application for permission to appeal which was granted permission: the case of *Oni*.[98] In that case, one of the applicants (Adedeji) was granted permission to adduce fresh evidence that another person (Numa) had, after trial, identified himself (Numa) as being the person in a video that had been used in evidence to convict Adedeji. He was granted permission to appeal, and his conviction was quashed the following year.[99] In statistical terms, therefore, the 75% success rate of fresh evidence in appeals that have been granted permission can hardly be considered overly tolerant of risk. But it is evidently difficult to receive permission to appeal. It is, therefore, important to consider whether this fact, and the cases behind that fact, evidences an approach which puts applicants (in particular) at unacceptable risk.

Before doing so, however, it is fruitful to consider some of the appeals that were allowed. The case of *Peterkin; Mehmet*,[100] a CCRC referral, concerned two appellants who had been convicted of conspiracy to steal following a trial in 1977. In 1980, three police officers who had investigated the case (Ridgewell, Ellis, and Keeling) had pleaded guilty to conspiracy to steal.[101]

97 *R v Falcon* [2024] EWCA Crim 311; *R v Reynolds* [2024] EWCA Crim 317; *R v Crane* [2024] EWCA Crim 312.

98 *R v Oni* [2024] EWCA Crim 893.

99 *R v Oni and others* [2025] EWCA Crim 12.

100 *R v Peterkin* [2024] EWCA Crim 309.

101 Those same officers had been implicated in numerous other appeals against conviction, see: *R v Simmons* [2018] EWCA Crim 114; *R v Trew, Christie and Griffiths* [2019] EWCA Crim 2474; *R v Boucher* [2020] EWCA Crim 629; *R v Geen, Harriott and Davidson* [2021] EWCA Crim 1026; *R v Johnson* [2021] EWCA Crim 1837. See also *R v Campbell* [2025] EWCA Crim 1146, concerning the same officers but occurring after the instant case.

Those convictions fatally undermined the integrity of the officers and the British Transport Police. Those convictions were admitted by the Court as fresh evidence and the appeal was allowed, it expressing both its regret at the delay and referring to the convictions as an injustice.[102] While it cannot be said with certainty that these appellants were innocent, the new evidence clearly increased the plausibility of that assertion; the appeal had to be allowed.

Gaiziunas[103] concerned an appellant who had been convicted of having a bladed article. The arresting officer said he found the knife in the appellant's briefcase; the appellant's case was that the knife had been planted there by the officer, and that the officer had also assaulted him. After conviction, the officer was convicted of ABH and perverting the course of justice (not related to this appellant). The officer's disciplinary record also noted concerned about the officer, both pre- and post-dating the appellant's convictions. The Court admitted this as fresh evidence and quashed the conviction because the officer's honesty and integrity were central to the case.[104] 'The appellant's persistent determination to see justice done', the Court said, 'is commendable and it has paid off'.[105] Again, the fresh evidence sufficiently increased the plausibility of the appellant's case.

In *Somers* the appellant had been convicted of handling stolen goods.[106] The allegation was that the complainant had been robbed of his Sur-Ron electric motorcycle. Two hours later, a police officer saw an electric motorcycle being ridden alongside a Seat Leon car belonging to the appellant. Inside the car was paperwork and accessories related to the Sur-Ron motorcycle. The appellant (eventually) admitted he was driving the car, but said that the motorcycle he had been seen driving alongside was not the Sur-Ron, and that he had no knowledge of the paperwork in the car. The appellant's phone was seized from him in April 2023 and returned to his mother in November 2023 (after conviction). On that phone were video clips recorded by the appellant of the incident, showing that the motorcycle he was driving alongside was not the Sur-Ron, just as he had said at trial. How it was that the police failed to notice this themselves is not commented upon in the judgment. For all intents and purposes it would appear that the appellant was innocent and exonerated of that particular crime. The Court admitted the recordings as fresh evidence and quashed the conviction.

There are some points to note about these appeals in the context of risk. None of these cases received any comment, or even acknowledgement, at all amongst academics (although the *Peterkin* case did receive some media coverage).[107] It is obvious why – they are not legally particularly interesting cases. But one does wonder how the claim of general narrowness can be sustained without

102 *Peterkin* (n 100) 20 and 23.
103 *R v Gaiziunas* [2024] EWCA Crim 246.
104 *R v Gaiziunas* [2024] EWCA Crim 19.
105 *R v Gaiziunas* [2024] EWCA Crim 22.
106 *R v Somers* [2024] EWCA Crim 1767.
107 Eg https://www.bbc.co.uk/news/uk-68017926

detailed knowledge of all the appeals that appear before the Court, including the rather legally uninteresting and routine ones such as these. It is suggested that the aforementioned cases do serve to undermine that suggestion. In the terms of risk employed by this book, while it might not be able to say with certainty that these appellants were innocent, the fresh evidence increased the plausibility of the appellant's cases. There was, therefore, more than enough doubt to mean that upholding the conviction would have placed the appellants at unacceptable risk. It is submitted that the Court was here robustly protecting the appellants from that risk.

Appeals dismissed

In *Wills*[108] the appellant sought to overturn his conviction for possessing a firearm with intent. The appellant's case at trial was self-defence, in which he said he waved an air-rifle at a council tax collection officer in the mistaken belief that the worker was a member of a gang who might have been out to kill him. The jury, obviously, rejected this assertion of self-defence. The proffered fresh evidence was that two months after trial the appellant had received an *Osman* warning – a threat to life warning issued by the police. That evidence, the Court said, was capable of belief, would have been admissible, and there was a reasonable explanation for not adducing the warning at trial, and so the only question was whether it would afford any ground for allowing the appeal.[109] The Court refused to admit the evidence on this final point, because the *Osman* warning had no impact on the appellant's actions, because it was not in existence when he threatened the council worker.[110] The appeal was accordingly dismissed.

It is submitted that on its facts this decision does appear harsh and the reasoning is suspect. The Court said that the new evidence regarding the *Osman* warning 'has no impact at all' because it was not something known to the appellant at the time he confronted the council worker.[111] But the defendant's case at trial, and all through the case from the point of arrest, was that he believed, or was concerned, that the worker could have been from a criminal gang with which he had previously been associated. The Court's use of the word 'impact' implies the *Pendleton* jury impact test, but the Court did not refer to that case. The Court does not need to protect appellants from all risk, but it is difficult to see how the fact of the *Osman* warning might not have been reasonably capable of bolstering the plausibility of his defence. In this particular decision, the appellant was arguably not protected from unacceptable risk. It is important, however, not to overstate

108 *R v Wills* [2024] EWCA Crim 1351.
109 *R v Wills* [2024] EWCA Crim 19.
110 *R v Wills* [2024] EWCA Crim 34.
111 *R v Wills* [2024] EWCA Crim 34.

the case; the appellant was not necessarily innocent and the Court was more aware of the facts than any outside observer could ever be. While the Court's assessment was perhaps unduly tolerant of risk, generally the Court was not unduly tolerant. This is considered in more detail in the context of renewed applications for permission.

The case of *Winter; Winter,*[112] a CCRC referral, concerned owners of a firework factory that exploded in 2006. Two emergency responders were killed, and the appellants were convicted of gross negligence manslaughter. The allegation was that the appellants had failed to properly store and handle explosives in accordance with the terms of their licence.[113] The appellants' cases were that they were not storing a particularly dangerous kind of firework (categorised as an HT1 firework) in the container and so were not liable. The appellants sought to adduce fresh evidence in the form of a letter and a circular from the Health and Safety Executive which they said undermined the claim that HT1 fireworks must have caused the explosions.[114] The Court rejected this argument by saying this argument 'focuses only on what is new. It fails to take into account what evidence there was before the jury at trial'.[115] The Court went on to say that the proposed fresh evidence could not have any appreciable impact on the cumulative effect of the prosecution evidence and dismissed the appeal.[116] In this case, in contrast perhaps to the prior case, the Court gave the evidence a detailed and holistic review. It is impossible in this particular case to say that the Court did not properly consider the evidence or that the appellants were not protected from unacceptable risk.

Renewed applications adducing fresh evidence

As discussed previously, the Law Commission was concerned that the Court would sometimes treat the considerations in section 23(2) as requirements rather than merely considerations.[117] The present study of cases from 2024 affirms that the Court would at times treat the considerations as criteria for admission. In *P*[118] the Court explicitly referred to the conditions in subsection (2) but did not refer at all (including when it set out 'the law' relating to fresh evidence at paragraph [34] of the judgment) to the interests of justice test in subsection (1).[119] The

112 *R v Winter* [2024] EWCA Crim 711.
113 *R v Winter* [2024] EWCA Crim 13.
114 *R v Winter* [2024] EWCA Crim 45.
115 *R v Winter* [2024] EWCA Crim 49.
116 *R v Winter* [2024] EWCA Crim 54.
117 See Law Commission (n 96) [6.61].
118 *R v P* [2024] EWCA Crim 488.
119 The judgment does make ample reference the 'interests of justice', but that is in the context of the interests of justice in granting an extension in light of the delay, not to the admission of the fresh evidence.

same happened in *Ward*;[120] *Tams*;[121] and *Brown*,[122] in which there was no reference to the interests of justice test. On the other hand, in cases such as *AFH*;[123] *Hussain*;[124] *Letby*;[125] and *Essien*[126] the Court referred to the considerations as mere considerations and the interests of justice test as being the test. There is therefore inconsistent practice. Those appeals which do not refer to the interests of justice test might give the *appearance*[127] of the Court applying the wrong test, and so some reform in this area might be beneficial.[128]

Given that the considerations are sometimes treated as criteria rather than mere considerations, how the Court considers those criteria is important. One of the suppositions offered by the Commission was that rather than consider whether the fresh evidence is 'capable of belief' (the wording of section 23(2)(a)) the Court in effect considers whether it believes the evidence.[129] There is (conceptually) a difference: not believing something does not mean that it is not *capable* of belief. The former question seems more difficult to satisfy, and would seem to require the Court to step into territory that (so the Court says often) belongs to the jury.[130] Reading the sample of cases from 2024 affirms the view that the Court does appear at times to consider not whether the evidence is capable of belief, but whether it believes it. This is, on the face of it, problematic.

However, the point should not be overstated. While there is a difference between the assessment of whether some fresh evidence is capable of belief and whether the Court believes it, that difference is slight. On the facts of most applications for permission, it is difficult to say that the Court would routinely dismiss evidence that was, on any view, capable of belief, despite the fact that it appears to approach the question from a perspective of whether it believed it itself. In truth, most of the fresh evidence that sought to be adduced came nowhere close to satisfying the overall test for admission. While the Court did often refuse to admit evidence following consideration of factor (a), it was actually factor (b) which was far more potent. Thus, it is difficult to say the Court routinely failed to protect appellants from unacceptable risk. Several cases from the pool of renewed applications are sufficient to illustrate the point.

120 *R v Ward* [2024] EWCA Crim 1696.
121 *R v Tams* [2024] EWCA Crim 582.
122 *R v Brown* [2024] EWCA Crim 426.
123 *R v AFH* [2024] EWCA Crim 1614 [29].
124 *R v Hussain* [2024] EWCA Crim 1223.
125 *R v Letby* [2024] EWCA Crim 748.
126 *R v Essien* [2024] EWCA Crim 598.
127 It is not suggested that the Court does not know what the correct test is, only that it might give the appearance of not knowing, or not wanting to apply that test.
128 See Chapter 4.
129 Law Commission (n 96) [6.109].
130 Indeed, as noted in chapter 1, one of the principal complaints about the Court is that it is too deferential towards the jury, i.e. it is unwilling to re-consider the evidence afresh. But in fresh evidence appeals that would appear to be what the Court does do.

Karim concerned an applicant who had been convicted of a joint enterprise robbery, and sought to adduce fresh evidence.[131] He denied presence at the scene of the robbery, and the case was circumstantial. The proffered fresh evidence was evidence from witnesses that a person referred to as X had taken the getaway car in order to implicate Karim as revenge for Karim informing on X to the police.[132] That suggestion was regarded by the single judge, with which the Court agreed, as 'preposterous' and not credible.[133] As explained in the judgement, the suggestion does appear entirely implausible, whether that is by an objective standard of credibility, or whether a Court could believe it. The applicant could have been innocent, but that would be contrary to the evidence in the case, and so the Court could hardly be considered too tolerant of the risk.

In *Cashman*[134] the Court set out the interests of justice test as being the test, before saying that for the evidence to be admissible it 'must be capable of belief'.[135] The Court said that 'no evidence is capable of belief if it is inherently fanciful'.[136] The proffered evidence, the Court thought, was fanciful and it explained convincingly the number of coincidences that had to have occurred for the evidence to be capable of belief.[137] The Court here was talking in these terms of relative plausibility, and clearly thought that the prosecution's version was more plausible. That is a justifiable application of the standard of proof. While the Court here quite clearly did not believe that the evidence was credible, it is impossible to say that the Court would have been wrong if it had simply said it was not capable of belief. To that extent, therefore, it can hardly be considered that the Court was not correctly applying the tests and protecting the applicant from unacceptable risk.

Most often, the application of the section 23(2) considerations turned on whether the Court was satisfied that the fresh evidence would afford a ground for allowing the appeal (consideration (b)). Thus in *Letby* the Court thought that the fresh expert evidence was credible but could not afford a ground for allowing the appeal.[138] In *Brown*[139] the Court accepted that the evidence was capable of belief. In order to consider whether the fresh evidence may afford a ground for allowing the appeal the Court said, (citing *Burridge*)[140] it must

131 *R v Karim* [2024] EWCA Crim 1773.
132 *R v Karim* [2024] EWCA Crim 17.
133 *R v Karim* [2024] EWCA Crim 18.
134 *R v Cashman* [2024] EWCA Crim 1543.
135 *R v Cashman* [2024] EWCA Crim 30.
136 *R v Cashman* [2024] EWCA Crim 30.
137 *R v Cashman* [2024] EWCA Crim 34–35.
138 *R v Letby* [2024] EWCA Crim 748 [191].
139 *Brown* (n 122).
140 *R v Burridge* [2010] EWCA Crim 2847. (*Burridge* was itself citing the case of *Dial* [2005] 1 WLR 1660).

'evaluate its importance in the context of the remainder of the evidence in the case'.[141] The Court provided a cogent analysis of the evidence and concluded that it would not provide a ground for allowing the appeal and so refused permission to appeal.

Other cases

There are two other cases which require some special consideration in relation to the Court's assessment of risk. Firstly, *Letby*. The consequences, if the Court's tolerance of risk is wrong, could not be more stark: either the Court risks an innocent nurse remaining imprisoned for the rest of her natural life, or it risks releasing a serial murderer of babies. Letby's case appeared twice before the Court in 2024, both as renewed applications. The second case (in October)[142] has been discussed above and concerned a relatively discrete issue around whether the second trial should have been stayed. The first application (in July)[143] was more wide-ranging.

She sought, amongst other things, to adduce fresh evidence to dispute the prosecution evidence regarding the cause of death of some of the babies.[144] The Court noted that in *Erskine* the Court had said that the factors in section 23(2) of the 1968 Act were neither exhaustive nor conclusive, with the focus being on the interest of justice test in section 23(1).[145] The Court doubted there was a reasonable explanation for not adducing the evidence at trial:[146]

> [No] good reason has been shown why the applicant should now be allowed to adduce evidence which could have been obtained and adduced at the appropriate time. The interests of justice require a defendant's whole case to be put forward at trial unless there is good reason why that could not be done.

This statement, taken in isolation, could be taken to support the view of the Law Commission that the Court is too impressed by the argument that some appellants might keep some evidence 'in reserve' to deploy at appeal.[147] However, this is not the main reason that the Court rejected the evidence. It went on to say that the fresh evidence did not provide a ground for allowing the appeal because it did not undermine the prosecution evidence.[148] The Court's

141 *R v Brown* (n 122) 33.
142 *Letby* (n 84).
143 *R v Letby* [2024] EWCA Crim 748.
144 *R v Letby* [2024] EWCA Crim 172–177.
145 *R v Letby* [2024] EWCA Crim 179.
146 *R v Letby* [2024] EWCA Crim 186.
147 See Law Commission (n 196) [6.85].
148 *Letby* (n 143) 190–191.

reasoning seemed comprehensive, but the issues at stake are highly complex. It is currently unknowable whether in the future the Court's decision in 2024 will be found to have been the wrong one and that she was not protected from unacceptable risk. It is important for the Court, in the future should the matter arise again, to recall that its role is to protect the appellant from that unacceptable risk, and that requires careful and sympathetic analysis of the plausibility of all the evidence.

The final case is *Hayes; Palombo,* a CCRC referral.[149] The case concerned two appellants convicted for their role in an alleged plan to manipulate the LIBOR and EURIOR rates.[150] The prosecution case was that Mr Hayes had been dishonest because the interest rates he had submitted to set LIBOR rates were not genuine assessments of the interest rate but instead based on commercial interests. The appeal was based whether the trial judge was right to direct the jury that, as a matter of law, a submission of an interest rate could not be genuine or honest if the person making it had taken any account of his commercial interests.[151] *Palombo* also relied on a case decided by the United States Court of Appeals for the Second Circuit (*Connelly and Black*),[152] in which similar convictions were quashed by the US court. Another issue that arose in this appeal was whether the grounds raised were related to the reasons the CCRC gave for making the reference, and if not whether the Court should grant leave to appeal.[153] A further issue was that the appellants had already made the same complaints in both an interlocutory appeal[154] and earlier appeal against conviction.[155] All previous ruling were negative to the appellants and so the question of *stare decisis* also fell to be considered by the Court.[156]

In the event, the Court concluded that most of the grounds of appeal raised were not related to the reasons given by the CCRC, and so it did not give leave to pursue them.[157] Further, the case of *Connolley and Black* did not cause 'us any doubt about the correctness of the English decisions as to the construction of LIBOR as a matter of English law, or by extension, of EURIBOR'.[158] Finally, *stare decisis* would have prevented the Court from allowing the appeal in any event because the point had already been addressed in five previous cases.[159] The appeals were therefore dismissed.

149 *R v Hayes* [2024] EWCA Crim 304.
150 Loosely, these are mechanisms which set the rates at which banks lend to each other.
151 *Hayes* (n 149) 79.
152 *United States v Connolly and Black* No. 19–3806.
153 *Hayes* (n 149) 83.
154 *R v H* [2015] EWCA Crim 46.
155 *R v Hayes* [2015] EWCA Crim 1944.
156 *Hayes* (n 149) 85–85.
157 *Hayes* (n 149) 118, 123.
158 *Hayes* (n 149) 114.
159 *Hayes* (n 149) 117.

What is more interesting is what happened afterwards: the appellants appealed to the UK Supreme Court and the convictions were quashed.[160] The Supreme Court was critical of the Court of Appeal's handling of the case. The Supreme Court said that the case 'raises concerns about the effectiveness of the criminal appeal system in England and Wales in confronting legal error'.[161] The Supreme Court accused the Court of Appeal of summarily rejecting the appellant's contentions that 'honesty' was a question of fact, not law.[162] The trial judge had been wrong to direct the jury that the rate submitted could not be honest or genuine if the submitter took account of any commercial interests of the bank or trader.[163] The Court of Appeal's rejection of that argument was flawed.[164] This is a case in which the Court's decision was wrong, because a higher Court had said so. It is therefore self-evident that the Court did not adequately protect these appellants. This represents a serious blunder by the Court of Appeal and may well call into question the Court's resolve to protect appellants from unacceptable risk. As said previously, in general the Court does appear to adequately protect appellants; the Supreme Court's warning should hopefully remind the Court that this is its task.

Summary

In summary, reading the Court's routine decisions discloses that it is difficult to say that the Court fails to protect appellants from unacceptable risk. It has to be said that most appellants did not directly put the question of their guilt / innocence into question. Instead, most asked the Court whether an alleged error by the trial judge constituted a procedural irregularity that rendered the conviction unsafe. When, as is usual, that question was answered in the negative, most appellants had no plausible claim of innocence or that there was any significant likelihood that they were innocent. It should be recalled that appellants appearing before the Court have already had a chance to avoid being convicted, and that was the trial. At trial, the appellant enjoyed the high standard of proof that was provided at trial, but the jury was sure that the appellant was guilty. While (as has been said) any number of appellant could in fact be innocent, the Court cannot quash convictions merely on account of that fact. This discussion of the Court's routine decisions shows why: any appellant could be innocent, but few were able to adduce any plausible explanation for the evidence against them that was accepted by the jury. In these conditions,

160 [2025] UKSC 29.
161 [2025] UKSC 1.
162 [2025] UKSC 4.
163 [2025] UKSC 8.
164 [2025] UKSC 158.

the Court would be doing more than necessary if it were to quash convictions to protect them from the risk of wrongful conviction.

Moreover, it is important to acknowledge that amongst the unsuccessful appeals, that raised the risk of perpetuating injustice, there is ample evidence of the Court correcting injustice. By this analysis there were several miscarriages of justice that were corrected at the first attempt by the Court in 2024. This should not be overlooked or downplayed. The most consistent allegation made against the Court is that its allegedly unduly narrow approach causes it to perpetuate miscarriages of justice. There is no clear evidence to support that allegation from this sample of appeals from 2024. But there is evidence, direct and incontrovertible, of the Court protecting appellants from the unacceptable risk of injustice when there is some plausible evidence in that direction. That, it is submitted, is all that can be asked of the Court and the Court largely complies with that obligation.

In relation to fresh evidence, there were identifiable difficulties with some aspects of its decision-making. But once again that should not be overstated. Adducing fresh evidence does not automatically mean that the fresh evidence is of any value or mean that the appellant has any plausible claim to be at unacceptable risk of injustice such that the Court should step in. A fair reading of the Court's routine decisions discloses, it is suggested, that most fresh evidence appeals stretch credibility and were appropriately rejected by the Court. It may well be at some point in the future shown that the Court was wrong to dismiss some of these appeals and applications. That has happened numerous times, not least, for instance, in a case such as *Malkinson*,[165] referred to in Chapter 1. That would mean that the injustice of wrongful conviction was perpetuated, and the appellant might have suffered significant injustice. But that does not mean that at the time it was given the Court was wrong to decide as it did, or that it did not provide the protection against risk that it could be expected to provide. Appeals against conviction take place under uncertain conditions; the Court cannot know the truth, and it must determine which of the options available to it protect appellants from unacceptable risk. It is submitted that is what the Court generally does, and there is little evidence that the Court does not comply with that duty.

From a reform perspective, therefore, the Court appears to be doing all that can be reasonably asked of it: protecting appellants from unacceptable risk. There are some areas in which the Court's exercise of its powers would be useful, and these are considered in the next chapter.

Conclusion

The key theme of this book has been how the concept of risk and risk assessment maps onto the unsafety test exercised in the Court of Appeal in appeals

165 *R v Malkinson* [2023] EWCA Crim 954.

against conviction. It has been argued that from a normal risk assessment perspective, the unsafety test means that the Court is required to protect appellants from unacceptable risk, not from all risk. This is how risk and uncertainty are dealt with in everyday life, and is a reasonable standard to apply to the Court of Appeal. The study of appeals against conviction decided in 2024 tested that supposition by examining whether the Court did assess risk and whether its assessment appeared generally in accordance with the standard of protecting appellants from unacceptable risk.

It has been concluded that the Court does assess risk by considering how likely, or how plausible, the appellants' claim to be wrongly convicted was. This accords with the standard of proof at trial discussed in Chapter 2. It has also been found that the Court does generally protect appellants from unacceptable risk, and there is little evidence to the contrary. Most appellants do not come close to raising doubts or raising the supposition that they are at unacceptable risk. While evidence of difficulties in some areas was located, and some of the Court's reasoning in individual cases could be criticised it is submitted that in general the Court did protect from unacceptable risk. To that end, reform directed towards inducing the Court to quash more convictions, or to be more liberal or less tolerant of risk is not necessary and will not be effective. Reforms may be helpful to clarify the Court's powers and to codify its role. Those are considered in the next chapter.

References

Anon, 'Ill-treatment of a Patient' 10 *Archbold Review* 3.

Benn, A, 'Causing a Public Nuisance' (2025) 1 *Criminal Law Review* 45

Chen, C, 'A Missed Opportunity to Correct the Law on Indecent Assault against Children' (2025) 89 (6) *Journal of Criminal Law* 349

Court of Appeal, *Annual Report 2023–2024*, https://www.judiciary.uk/wp-content/uploads/2025/01/24.278_JO_A_Review_of_the_Year_In_the_Court_of_Appeal_Criminal_Division_2023-24_WEB.pdf

Dargue, P, 'An Analysis of Disclosure Failings in Murder Appeals Against Conviction' (2020) *Criminal Law Review* 707

Dargue, P, 'The Safety of Convictions in the Court of Appeal: Fresh Evidence in the Criminal Division through an Empirical Lens' (2019) 83 (6) *Journal of Criminal Law* 433

Dargue, P, 'The Tolerability of Risk in the Court of Appeal (Criminal Division): An Empirical Study of Appeals against Conviction' (2025) 12 *Criminal Law Review* 743

DPP v Rogers (1953) 37 Cr App R 137

Fairclough v Whipp (1951) 35 Cr App R 138

Hungerford-Welch, P, 'Ill-Treatment of a Person in Care' (2025) 2 *Criminal Law Review* 102

Knight, M, *Criminal Appeals* (Stephen and Sons, 1970)

Law Commission, *Criminal Appeals: Consultation Paper* (Law Comm No 268, 2025)

Mackay, R, 'Fitness to Plead' (2024) 8 *Criminal Law Review* 576
Malleson, K, *The Royal Commission on Criminal Justice Research Study No 17* (HMSO, 1993)
Parpworth, N, 'Public Nuisance and the Meaning of a "Section of the Public"' (2025) 89 (1) *Journal of Criminal Law* 52
R v AAB [2024] EWCA Crim 880
R v ADD and others [2022] EWCA Crim 106
R v AFH [2024] EWCA Crim 1614 [29]
R v AJJ and others [2021] EWCA Crim 1278
R v Ali [2024] EWCA Crim 77
R v BAA [2024] EWCA Crim 343
R v Ben Smith [2024] EWCA Crim 342
R v BJK [2024] EWCA Crim 667
R v BJS [2024] EWCA Crim 1356
R v BNN [2024] EWCA Crim 991
R v Brooker [2024] EWCA Crim 103
R v Brown [2024] EWCA Crim 426
R v Burridge [2010] EWCA Crim 2847
R v BVY [2024] EWCA Crim 1355
R v Cashman [2024] EWCA Crim 1543
R v Crane [2024] EWCA Crim 312
R v Davis, Rowe, and Johnson [2001] 1 Cr App R 8
R v Dundon [2004] EWCA Crim 621
R v Dunn [2015] EWCA Crim 724
R v Essien [2024] EWCA Crim 598
R v F [2024] EWCA Crim 463
R v Falcon [2024] EWCA Crim 311
R v FGH [2024] EWCA Crim 1353
R v Fisher [2024] EWCA Crim 1605
R v Gaiziunas [2024] EWCA Crim 246
R v Galbraith [2024] EWCA Crim 1148
R v H [2015] EWCA Crim 46
R v Hanna [2024] EWCA Crim 1315
R v Hayes [2015] EWCA Crim 1944
R v Hayes [2024] EWCA Crim 304
R v Hayes [2025] UKSC 29
R v Head [2024] EWCA Crim 1487
R v Heaven [2024] EWCA Crim 88
R v Hill [2024] EWCA Crim 1423
R v Hussain [2024] EWCA Crim 1223
R v Ismail [2024] EWCA Crim 301
R v Jodeiri-Lakpour [2024] EWCA Crim 97
R v Joshua Smith [2024] EWCA Crim 1040
R v Karim [2024] EWCA Crim 1773
R v Kent [2024] EWCA Crim 1271
R v Khan [2024] EWCA Crim 148
R v Kutek [2024] EWCA Crim 1675
R v Letby [2024] EWCA Crim 748

R v Letby [2024] EWCA Crim 1278
R v LMS [2024] EWCA Crim 96
R v Malkinson [2023] EWCA Crim 954
R v Mark Smith [2024] EWCA Crim 390
R v Matthew Banner; R v Peter Bennett [2024] EWCA Crim 1201
R v McNaughton [2024] EWCA Crim 1129
R v Menzies [2024] EWCA Crim 1549
R v Mundle [2024] EWCA Crim 1289
R v N [2024] EWCA Crim 489
R v Oni [2024] EWCA Crim 893
R v Oni and others [2025] EWCA Crim 12
R v P [2024] EWCA Crim 488
R v Peterkin [2024] EWCA Crim 309
R v Reid [2024] EWCA Crim 308 [35]
R v Reynolds [2024] EWCA Crim 317
R v Serdoud [2024] EWCA Crim 1398
R v Somers [2024] EWCA Crim 1767
R v Tams [2024] EWCA Crim 582
R v Togher [2001] 3 All ER 463
R v TT [2024] EWCA Crim 616
R v Ward [2024] EWCA Crim 1696
R v Wills [2024] EWCA Crim 1351
R v Wilson [2024] EWCA Crim 1514
R v Winter [2024] EWCA Crim 711
R v Zulfiqar and others [2024] EWCA Crim 1710
Roberts, S, 'Fresh Evidence and Factual Innocence in the Criminal Division of the Court of Appeal' (2017) 81 (4) *Journal of Criminal Law* 303
Sjolin, C, 'The Need to Kill off Zombie Law: Indecent Assault, Where It Went Wrong and How to Put It Right' (2017) 81 *Journal of Criminal Law* 50
United States v Connolly and Black No. 19-3806
Wadham, J, Mountfield, H, Prochaska, E, Desai, R, *Blackstone's Guide to the Human Rights Act 1998* (7th edn, Oxford University Press, 2015)

4 Proposals for reform

Introduction

This chapter will be broadly based around the Law Commission's consultation questions in which numerous proposals for revision to the powers and the processes of the Court were made. In the spirit of consultation question 108 (an invitation to give views on any other relevant issues not otherwise addressed) this chapter makes some recommendations which are not found in the consultation questions. In accordance with the earlier chapters of this book, it is argued that reform should not be targeted towards inducing a more liberal approach, because it cannot be properly said that there is any flaw with its approach. Instead, the unsafety test should be amended to better reflect the issue of risk, in order to ensure that the Court understands its role of protecting appellants from unacceptable risk.

The Law Commission's proposals

The Law Commission's terms of reference in its consultation into the criminal appeal system were to 'consider the need for reform with a view to ensuring that the courts have powers that enable the effective, efficient and appropriate resolution of appeals'.[1] It considered all aspects of the criminal appeal system, including some that are beyond the scope of this book and so no detailed discussion is made of them.[2] The parts most relevant to this book were the parts which reviewed the Court of Appeal's decision-making, the unsafety test, and the Court's approach towards the unsafety test and fresh evidence. In relation to the unsafety test the Commission was asked to consult on 'whether there is evidence which suggests that the test for allowing an appeal on the grounds that a conviction is unsafe may hinder the correction of miscarriages

1 Law Commission, *Criminal Appeals: Consultation Paper* (Law Comm No 268, 2025) [1.5].

2 For example, the Law Commission examined in depth the Criminal Cases Review Commission, but this book has had almost nothing to say on the CCRC as an institution.

DOI: 10.4324/9781003782292-5

of justice'.[3] To address that question the Commission was to pay particular regard to the Court's approach towards fresh evidence and 'lurking doubt' appeals and to consider the need for reform.

The relevant principles

To consider whether reform was necessary, the Commission proposed (consultation question 3)[4] that the relevant principles are:

1) The acquittal of the innocent
2) The conviction of the guilty
3) Fairness
4) Recognising the role of the jury on indictment
5) Upholding the integrity of the criminal justice system
6) Ensuring access to justice
7) Finality

As has been discussed, the Commission could not find significant fault with the unsafety test. But it was concerned that in places the Court's approach was too narrow.[5] The Commission's answer to the question of whether there is evidence to suggest that the *test* hinders the remedy of miscarriages of justice can be fairly said to be 'no', but that the Court's *approach* towards the test might hinder the remedy of miscarriages of justice. It is worth pausing to briefly consider in light of the aforementioned principles whether the question of 'hindering' the remedy of miscarriages of justice is a useful one. This book has argued that the Court's central function is to protect appellants from the unacceptable risk of injustice, but it cannot be expected to protect them from all risk. From this perspective, any 'approach' that permits the Court to uphold any conviction must be 'hindering' the remedy of miscarriages of justice, because there is a risk in any dismissed appeal that the Court could be perpetuating a miscarriage of justice.

If the purpose of reform is to prevent the Court 'hindering' the remedy of miscarriages of justice, that would seem a nearly impossible task. The real purpose of reform should be to enable the Court to perform the overriding objective of dealing with cases justly, which includes remedying the conviction of the innocent, and quashing convictions that ought to be quashed, but also upholding the conviction of the guilty and the properly convicted. The Court cannot be reasonably expected to perform its task perfectly; instead it should protect from the unacceptable risk of injustice so that it is as low as reasonably

3 Law Commission (n 1) [1.5].
4 Law Commission (n 1) [4.141].
5 Law Commission (n 1) [8.123].

practicable, not extinguished altogether. Accordingly, the Law Commission's seven principles are agreeable, but to those principles should be added the appropriate apportionment of the risk of injustice.

Question 17 – The admission of fresh evidence

The Court's handling of fresh evidence is one of the more contentious aspects of its decision-making. In relation to the admission of fresh evidence, the Commission expressed particular concern about factor (a): the need to consider whether the evidence is 'capable of belief'.[6] As discussed in Chapter 3, the Commission thought that the Court considers this factor narrowly and that its approach is to '[weigh] the fresh evidence against the other evidence in the trial [and] if, on balance, it prefers the other evidence, the fresh evidence is incapable of belief'.[7] It should be noted that '*capable* of belief' is the wording of the criteria in section 23(2)(a) of the Act; the criteria do not require (or, arguably, permit) the Court to consider whether it believes the evidence itself. If the Court finds that the evidence is not 'capable of belief' then it cannot be in the interests of justice to admit it (which, as noted, is the real test for admission).

The Commission asked in question 17:

> The test for admitting fresh evidence in section 23 of the Criminal Appeal Act 1968 should remain "in the interests of justice", provided that the considerations in subsection (2) are treated as such rather than as criteria which must be met before fresh evidence can be admitted. Do consultees agree?

This is an attempt to direct the Court away from dismissing appeals on the basis that the fresh evidence is allegedly not credible, and towards considering the overall interests of justice test. It is unclear what form this proposal would take and how it could have any legal effect. The Court will do what it is directed to do by statute, and if the statute requires consideration of the section 23(2) factors in determining whether it is in the interests of justice to admit the evidence then that is what the Court will do. It is unclear how the Court could be, as it were, 'reminded' that the factors are mere factors and not criteria which must be met. It is worth setting out the factors here, to consider whether they could be reformed to protect appellants from unacceptable risk. The factors in section 23(2) are:

(a) Whether the evidence appears to the Court to be capable of belief
(b) Whether it appears to the Court that the evidence may afford any ground for allowing the appeal

6 Law Commission (n 1) [6.109].
7 Law Commission (n 1) [6.73].

(c) Whether the evidence would have been admissible
(d) Whether there is a reasonable explanation for failure to adduce the evidence at trial

It is submitted that to protect appellants from unacceptable risk, the barriers to the admission of fresh evidence should be lowered. To that end, the wording of these factors are problematic. By use of the verb 'to be' in factor (a) the Court is required to consider whether the evidence *is* capable of belief. There is no way for the Court to realistically determine that question other than by asking itself whether it finds the evidence credible. (Note that at this stage the Court has not formally 'received' or heard the evidence). If the Court does not think that the evidence is capable of belief, then it seems impossible for it to be in the interests of justice to admit it, for the appeal could never be allowed. For the purpose of admission, it is submitted, the test should be lowered to whether the evidence 'may' be capable of belief. That form of wording would appear to lower the barrier for admission and so should permit more fresh evidence to pass this filter and potentially be admitted and considered in light of the unsafety test.

Factor (b) is also problematic because it requires the Court to consider whether the conviction would be unsafe, before formally admitting the evidence. It is submitted that this factor adds little to the unsafety test but does narrow the avenues for admission. Again the legislature placed the Court in an impossible position; the Court cannot consider (b) without also considering the unsafety test. It should, therefore be deleted in its entirety. The Court should put the unsafety test 'out of its mind' when it is considering the admissibility considerations, but the only way to do that is deletion of factor (b). Factor (c) is unproblematic.

Consideration (d) is problematic. The grounds for criticism are that it leaves open the prospect that credible, potentially exculpatory, evidence would not be admitted because there was not a reasonable explanation for not the appellant not being aware of it at the time of trial.[8] However, it is submitted that there is an element of unreality about some of this criticism. It is very rare for the Court to refuse to admit evidence purely on the basis of factor (d).[9] It is unthinkable that the Court would find the admission of fresh *credible,* exculpatory evidence not to be in the interests of justice only on grounds of factor (d). It is submitted that, since the question of the admission of fresh evidence in any event only comes into play if the evidence is considered 'fresh', the need for factor (d) is unclear. It should therefore be removed from the factors altogether.

8 Law Commission (n 1) [6.78–87].
9 See P Dargue, 'The Tolerability of Risk in the Court of Appeal (Criminal Division): An Empirical Study of Appeals against Conviction' (2025) 12 *Criminal Law Review* 743.

It is proposed, therefore, that section 23 be amended so that the Court can receive fresh evidence if in the interests of justice, and it should consider whether a) the evidence may be capable of belief and b) whether the evidence is admissible. Once the evidence has been admitted, which, it is suggested, might now occur more often, the Court will need to consider whether the conviction is unsafe. It is at the stage of assessing unsafety that the Court will go on to consider the question of risk.

Question 34 – The unsafety test

The Law Commission asked:

> The single ground that a conviction is unsafe should continue to be the test for quashing a conviction, but that the circumstances in which a conviction will be unsafe should be set out non-exhaustively in legislation. We provisionally propose that these circumstances should include the following, which we consider represent the current practice of the Court of Appeal Criminal Division: (1) where the Court considers that the appellant's trial, as a whole, was unfair; or (2) where the Court considers that the conviction of the appellant involved abuse of process amounting to an affront to justice. Do consultees agree?

It is submitted that this proposal should be accepted but only in part. The Commission concluded that 'unsafety' should remain the test; it is submitted that the Commission are correct about that. It is difficult to think of any other word that would serve the purposes better than the current word. As has been discussed, it fits well within a system that seeks to apportion risk, and the Court's function of protecting appellants from unacceptable risk. However, the proposal to set out some of the circumstances in which a conviction will be unsafe should not be accepted. There are several reasons for this. The Court well understands that the two proposed circumstances (shown earlier) must render convictions unsafe. It would add little to codify those circumstances into the statute. It should also be noted that the two proposed circumstances are narrow components of the unsafety test. There is a danger that if they are put in statute the Court may consider it is *only* in those circumstances in which a conviction can be unsafe. This is, obviously, not what the Commission intend but could be a consequence.

It is submitted that the Court could receive more guidance about what constitutes an unsafe conviction. The overriding duty of the Court is to satisfy the 'overriding objective' to deal with cases justly. This ought to be included in the statute, otherwise that duty may no longer appear 'overriding'. It has been argued in this book that the unsafety test is an example of risk taking under uncertain conditions and, as such, ordinary principles of risk assessment apply. This means that a conviction is safe when there is freedom from unacceptable risks. It should therefore be explained when there is an unacceptable risk, and to that end *Pearson*[10] should be codified. It is proposed that section 2 of the 1968 Act be re-drafted along the following lines:

2 The Court –

(1) (a) shall allow an appeal if they think that the conviction is unsafe; and (b) shall dismiss the appeal otherwise

(2) In the case of an appeal against conviction the Court shall, if they allow the appeal, quash the conviction.

(3) An order of the Court of Appeal quashing a conviction shall, except when under section 7 below the appellant is ordered to be retried, operate as a direction to the court of trial to enter, instead of the record of conviction, a judgment and verdict of acquittal.

(4) A conviction is unsafe if there is an unacceptable risk of injustice, taking into account the overriding objective of dealing with cases justly.

(5) There is an unacceptable risk to justice when:

   (a) It appears someone other than the appellant may have committed the offence
   (b) The conviction is vitiated by unfairness or legal irregularity
   (c) The Court is not sure the jury would still have convicted had it known everything about the case that the Court now knows
   (d) The Court is otherwise concerned that an injustice might have been done

It is submitted that re-drafting the unsafety test in this way would have a number of benefits. The unsafety test remains the primary test and there is no attempt to reduce the protective scope of the test. By requiring the Court to express that it has considered the risk and considers the risk to be acceptable / unacceptable, the Court is properly taking account of the uncertainty of the situation. It is a more frank and honest assessment of the situation in which the Court finds itself. Finally, the proposed wording would require the Court to state in open Court that they do not believe an injustice has been done (i.e. they do not have a lurking doubt), and explain why. How fresh evidence would fit into this scheme is now considered.

Question 35 – Assessment of fresh evidence

The Commission was concerned that the Court will 'often uphold a conviction on the basis that *it* is satisfied of the strength of the evidence against the appellant

10 *R v CCRC ex parte Pearson* [2000] 1 Cr App R 141.

without considering the potential effect of the evidence on a jury'.[11] (That is, once any fresh evidence has been admitted.) As discussed in Chapter 3, most appeals in that sample which raised fresh evidence were successful, which might diminish this point somewhat. However, fresh evidence was regularly rejected in applications for permission because the Court did not find the evidence credible and, in short, it was sure the appellant was guilty. Whether this is a problem or not might depend upon the degree of risk from which the appellant ought to be protected. It was said in Chapter 3 that in many cases where fresh evidence was rejected by the Court, it appeared a fair rejection. It cannot be known whether the Court was right in that assessment in all the applications which were rejected; some of the unsuccessful applicants might have been innocent. But perfection cannot be expected, and it is quite difficult to say that the Court was not adequately protecting the applicants from unacceptable risk in the appeals sampled in Chapter 3.

It is on the basis of its concerns that the Commission made recommendation / question 35. This was:

> **Question 35:**
>
> We provisionally propose that where, in an appeal against conviction, the Court of Appeal Criminal Division admits fresh evidence that could have led the jury to acquit, then the Court should order a retrial unless a retrial is impossible or impractical. Do consultees agree?

The purpose of question 35 is somewhat unclear as presented in the report. There is currently no section within the Criminal Appeal Act 1968 / 1995 that directs the Court what to do with fresh evidence once admitted, other than section 2 which requires it to consider whether the conviction is unsafe. As noted above, the Commission considered the test for admission of fresh evidence under section 23 in question 17, so question 35 is not a proposal about further amendments to section 23. Question 34 related to retaining the unsafety test as the ground to allow appeals, so question 35 cannot (ostensibly) be a proposal about when fresh evidence should render a conviction unsafe. The omission of the words 'should quash the conviction' before 'should order a retrial' in question 35, might suggest that the proposal is only about increasing the use of retrials where appropriate. If that is the case then the proposal is acceptable, subject to the need to ensure that successful appellants are not placed at unacceptable risk of unwarranted (re)conviction by the ordering of a retrial.[12]

11 Law Commission (n 1) [8.113].

12 Some responses to the consultation seemed to infer that proposal 35 was only a call for more retrials, see for example response by the Law Society, https://www.lawsociety.org.uk/campaigns/consultation-responses/law-commission-consultation-on-criminal-appeals-july-2025 at 16.

It is unlikely that this is all that the Commission meant. In the context of its place in the report, the proposal appears to be an attempt to legislate an approach to fresh evidence. In its response to the consultation, the organisation APPEAL took the proposal to mean the enshrining of the 'jury impact test' in law when deciding whether the conviction is unsafe.[13] To that end, the appropriate place for the proposal might be in section 2; this also is what the Criminal Bar Association thought in their response.[14] If the aforementioned proposed redrafting of section 2 were to reach approval, the proposal in question 35 might add a section 2(5)(e) to the unsafety test:

> There is an unacceptable risk to justice when:
>
> . . .
>
> (e) The Court admits fresh evidence that could have led the jury to acquit

The Commission's question 35 was based on the Royal Commission on Criminal Justice (RCCJ) report which said that once the Court has admitted evidence that is relevant and capable of belief, and which could have affected the outcome of the case, it should quash the conviction and order a retrial.[15] It is worth pausing momentarily to acknowledge that in practice this is what the Court does at present when it applies *Pendleton.* If the Court finds that the fresh evidence could have affected the outcome of the case it will be inevitable that the conviction will be unsafe and will be quashed. At paragraph 8.114 of its report the Commission said that there are some cases where fresh evidence is admitted, and which might have made a difference to the jury's verdict, that are nevertheless upheld. It did not provide any examples. There is a difference between saying that a piece of fresh evidence might (theoretically) have impacted the jury's verdict, and saying that the Court *finds* the fresh evidence might have impacted the jury's verdict; in the latter case the conviction will be allowed according to the Court's current decision-making approach. The Commission was presumably talking of the former situation. But there are no cases where the Court finds the fresh evidence might have impacted the verdict that are then dismissed.[16]

13 See Appeal, Response to Law Commission Consultation, https://appeal.org.uk/wp-content/uploads/2025/07/APPEAL-response-to-Law-Commission-Consultation-Paper_June-2025.pdf at 15–16.

14 Criminal Bar Association, Response to Law Commission Consultation, https://www.criminalbar.com/wp-content/uploads/2025/07/CBA-Response-to-the-Law-Commission-Consultation-%E2%80%98Criminal-Appeals.pdf at 26.

15 Discussed by the Law Commission (n 1) at [8.126].

16 If this is incorrect, and there are some cases in the record, they may be an anomaly or decided on its particular facts.

With respect, the wording of the proposal in question 35 should not be accepted. Taken exactly as written in the report, it does not require any consideration of the plausibility of the proffered evidence when considering whether the conviction is rendered unsafe. One can assume that within proposal 35 the Commission wanted to include some assessment of relevance and credibility along the lines stated by the RCCJ, so the proposal should have read:

> Where, in an appeal against conviction, the Court of Appeal Criminal Division admits fresh evidence that is *relevant and capable of belief* and could have led the jury to acquit, then the Court should order a retrial unless a retrial is impossible or impractical.

The proposed reformed section 2(5)(e) would now read that

> There is an unacceptable risk to justice when:
>
> . . .
>
> (e) The Court admits fresh evidence that is relevant and capable of belief and that could have led the jury to acquit

The problem with this provision, however, remains the words 'could have'. As discussed in Chapter 2, it is submitted that Hughes LJ's words in *Ahmed*[17] provide a significant obstacle. Since a jury has not seen the fresh evidence, any fresh evidence that is both relevant and credible 'could have' some impact on the jury. If an appellant can show that the fresh evidence could theoretically impact the verdict of the jury, it would seem that proposal 35 would require that the appeal is allowed. It is suggested that there must be some limit, because the Court is only required to protect an appellant from unacceptable risks, and seek to reduce that risk so it is as low as reasonably practicable. The appropriate limit, it is suggested, is that the Court must think the fresh evidence might 'plausibly' impact the verdict of the jury to convict. This would require convictions to be quashed when there is some plausible doubt about guilt caused by the fresh evidence, and so would protect the appellant from unacceptable risk, but would not require the quashing of all convictions.

Other matters

Composition

The analysis of the sample of appeals discussed in Chapter 3 has driven a number of conclusions around administrative matters in the Court. One observation

17 *R v Ahmed* [2010] EWCA Crim 2899.

is that most appeals are relatively simple. The great majority of appeals are focused on an appellant raising one or two procedural irregularities and inviting the Court to find that those irregularities did in fact occur and that they rendered the conviction unsafe. The prosecution will usually resist the claim that an irregularity occurred, or may accept that one did occur but argue it does not render the conviction unsafe. Chapter 3 affirmed that usually the Court will find that no such irregularity occurred and duly dismiss the appeal. As discussed in Chapter 3, it is often quite clear that the alleged irregularity did not occur, or rather, it would require a generous interpretation to say that an error did occur. This is, it is submitted, the reality in the routine workload of the Court.

Given this supposition that most appeals are relatively simple, it is at least questionable whether a bench of three judges is required for the majority of appeals, and in particular it is doubtful whether a Lord / Lady Justice is required for most appeals. There does not appear to be anything inherently wrong with a High Court judge (a different High Court judge to the judge who determined applications for permission) reviewing decisions of a circuit judge, for instance. It is suggested that the default position should be that appeals against conviction are to be determined by a High Court judge and another judge, either a Lord / Lady Justice, or a circuit judge, recorder, or retired High Court judge. If there is a dispute amongst the bench of two, the benefit should go to the appellant. It is suggested that it is only in a minority of appeals where a bench of three is necessary; for instance where there are particularly complex matters or a large number of grounds of appeal. It should be the registrar and / or the single judge at the permission stage who determines the number and composition of benches.

Since at present most appeals have at least one Lord / Lady Justice and a High Court judge the reduction in composition may free up judicial time. A reduction in the Court's battle against its workload would potentially allow for a more detailed and holistic approach. It is possible that given generally slightly looser workloads following this recommendation might induce a greater willingness to grant permission to appeal in the first place; this might, in turn, provide a greater level of protection against risk.

Applications for permission

The Criminal Appeal Act places no limit or exclusions on the grounds that can be raised by an appellant. Section 1 of the 1968 Act (as amended) gives the right to seek leave to appeal to all persons convicted on indictment, and the conviction is to be quashed if the Court thinks the conviction is unsafe. There is nothing else in the Act as to when a conviction will be unsafe. The need to adduce grounds is found in Part 39.3 of the Criminal Procedure Rules. But these merely state that the appellant must identify the event or decision to which the ground relates (39.3.(2)(b); must identify each ground of appeal (39.3(1)(b)); must outline the argument in support of each ground (39.3(2)(d)); and must identify any relevant authority (39.3(2)(f)). The Rules say nothing about the kinds of grounds that an appellant is permitted to adduce.

The *Blue Book* guide to commencing proceedings in the Court of Appeal states that grounds of appeal must be sufficiently particularised, and a ground that 'the conviction is unsafe' will be ineffective.[18] The closest one gets to a statement of what kinds of grounds should or should not be adduced is in the guidance document on completing form NG (the application for permission to appeal).[19] It says this:[20]

> An appeal against conviction is <u>not</u> another trial which looks again at the facts of the case in the way the jury did to decide if the appellant is guilty or innocent. The Court of Appeal will only be concerned with whether the conviction is unsafe and will consider issues such as: whether the trial as a whole was fair; whether the trial Judge made the correct legal rulings during the course of the trial; whether the trial Judge fairly summed up the case to the jury with the appropriate legal directions; "fresh evidence" that was not presented at trial.

This 'guidance' is quite unhelpful. There is nothing in the Criminal Appeal Acts that says an appeal is not a retrial, albeit that is the Court's practice. There is nothing in the Act that says the Court will not look at the facts of the case; indeed, as is well known, the Court does often explicitly look at the facts of the case. It is true that the Court will be concerned with the fairness of the trial and legal rulings, etc, and so to that extent the Court is not concerned about guilt or innocence. But if an appellant can adduce some doubt about guilt, up to and including – but not requiring – showing they are likely innocent, then the conviction must be unsafe. As such, whether the appellant is guilty or innocent is squarely relevant to the question of unsafety. Belief in guilt is a precondition of safety, and it is disingenuous to suggest otherwise. This is clear from all that was discussed earlier in this book: that justice requires as far as reasonably possible the acquittal of the innocent and the conviction of the guilty. Consequently, a convicted person is entitled *by law* to seek to appeal on the basis that they might be innocent and to require the Court to assess whether the risk of innocence is unacceptable; nothing in the Criminal Appeal Act suggests otherwise.

It is submitted that the guidance to appellants should be reconsidered and make it clear that the test to have an appeal allowed is whether the conviction

18 Judiciary of England and Wales, *The Court of Appeal Criminal Division Guide to Commencing Proceedings* (2021), https://www.judiciary.uk/wp-content/uploads/2021/07/Blue-guide-July-2021-Final-1.pdf at 2.

19 Judiciary, Guidance on Completing Form NG, https://assets.publishing.service.gov.uk/media/5fdb228d8fa8f54d60878b3b/ng-guidance.pdf

20 Judiciary (n 20) section H. (Emphasis original).

is safe or unsafe and that they are entitled to a verdict from the Court as to whether their own conviction is safe.

It is suggested that this small selection of recommendations for reform to the Court's processes would place the Court's decision-making on a surer legislative footing. By drawing the unsafety test into the orbit of risk and risk assessment, its core functions would be clearer. This, it is submitted, would help to ensure that the Court does protect appellants from unacceptable risk.

Conclusion

This chapter has examined the Law Commission's proposals for reform in so far as they relate to the Court's approach towards the unsafety test and fresh evidence. The study of the Court's judgments discussed in Chapter 3 ultimately concluded that criticism of the Court was overblown but that there were areas where reform would be beneficial. The proposals made in this chapter have sought to support the core thesis that the function of the Court is to protect the appellant from unacceptable risk, but that it need not protect from all risk. To that end, it was proposed that the unsafety test be re-constituted around the concept of risk, and *Pearson* be codified. The Court could be more liberal in the receipt and assessment of fresh evidence, and proposals in this direction have been suggested. Overall, the powers of the Court do not require significant revision, but should be brought into closer alignment with its core function to protect from unacceptable risk.

References

Appeal, Response to Law Commission Consultation, https://appeal.org.uk/wp-content/uploads/2025/07/APPEAL-response-to-Law-Commission-Consultation-Paper_June-2025.pdf

Criminal Bar Association, Response to Law Commission Consultation, https://www.criminalbar.com/wp-content/uploads/2025/07/CBA-Response-to-the-Law-Commission-Consultation-%E2%80%98Criminal-Appeals.pdf at 26

Dargue, P, 'The Tolerability of Risk in the Court of Appeal (Criminal Division): An Empirical Study of Appeals against Conviction' (2025) 12 *Criminal Law Review* 743

Judiciary of England and Wales, *The Court of Appeal Criminal Division Guide to Commencing Proceedings* (2021), https://www.judiciary.uk/wp-content/uploads/2021/07/Blue-guide-July-2021-Final-1.pdf

Judiciary of England and Wales, Guidance on Completing Form NG, https://assets.publishing.service.gov.uk/media/5fdb228d8fa8f54d60878b3b/ng-guidance.pdf

Law Commission, *Criminal Appeals: Consultation Paper* (Law Comm No 268, 2025)

Law Society, Response to Law Commission Consultation, https://www.lawsociety.org.uk/campaigns/consultation-responses/law-commission-consultation-on-criminal-appeals-july-2025

R v Ahmed [2010] EWCA Crim 2899

R v CCRC ex parte Pearson [2000] 1 Cr App R 141

Conclusion

Introduction

This concluding chapter summarises the book's key arguments and findings. It has been argued that the unsafety test operated by the Court of Appeal is best understood through the lens of risk. The Court takes a risk when it determines that a conviction is safe or unsafe. Since something is safe when there is freedom from unacceptable risk, it follows that the function of the Court is to protect appellants from unacceptable risks; however, it cannot be expected to protect from all risk. Overall, it is argued that the Court's approach towards this function is sensible and it cannot be said in any general sense that the Court fails to provide adequate protection. The development of this theoretical framework represents a novel and innovative way to examine the Court's decisions in appeals against conviction.

Taking risks in criminal appeals

As discussed in Chapter 1, the provenance of the concept of 'unsafety' in the context of criminal appeals is rather vague, yet it has been a feature of appeals against conviction since the enactment of the Criminal Appeal Act 1966, which was later consolidated by the Criminal Appeal Act 1968. The Criminal Appeal Act 1995 enacted the simple test that the Court is to allow and appeal, and so quash the conviction(s) if it thinks that the conviction is unsafe. This test has been in operation for thirty years and so is a well-entrenched part of the criminal appeal system. The reason for the adoption of the unsafety test was the perception that the Court's approach towards its powers was unduly cautious or narrow. Despite the adoption of the unsafety test, the Court has continued to receive strong criticism for its apparent approach. The fact that the Law Commission was asked recently to review the decision-making approach of the Court evidences continued concern regarding its approach. This was discussed in some detail in Chapter 1 of this book.

The concept of safety / unsafety in the context of criminal appeals maps closely onto the broader concept of risk. A risk is taken whenever there is

DOI: 10.4324/9781003782292-6

uncertainty regarding the consequences of an event with respect to something humans value.[1] It is thus uncertainty that gives rise to the necessity of taking a risk. In normal life, when one takes a risk one embarks upon an activity where there is the possibility of unwanted outcome. It is not possible to remove that risk from life, other than ceasing all activities that constitute the doing of life. More formal settings, such as decisions of the Parole Board and the activities of the Health and Safety Executive, demonstrate that perfection is not required when consequential decisions are taken. What is expected is a proper assessment of the risks, and due consideration of whether the residual risk is truly a risk that can be tolerated. It is in this context that something can be considered safe when there is freedom from unacceptable risk, meaning that the risk has been kept as low as reasonably practicable and the activity in question is worth the residual risk.

The Court of Appeal sits atop the criminal justice system in a supervisory capacity. The wider criminal justice also takes risks with respect to something humans value, namely: the doing of justice. Every person involved in the operation of the criminal process is required to act to achieve the overriding objective of dealing with cases justly. But it is not possible to know what needs to be done to achieve justice; the facts are uncertain. Consequently, in seeking to do justice there is a risk of doing injustice. As was discussed in Chapter 2, the most important risk taking part of the criminal process to this book, apart from the appeal system itself, is the Crown Court jury trial. The jury are to attempt to acquit the innocent and convict the guilty, but it is inevitable that on occasion the innocent will be convicted and the guilty acquitted. While this risk occurs in every case before every jury in England and Wales, jury trials (and, indeed, other trials) continue. They continue to function despite the possibility of mistake because the social value of convicting the guilty.

The Court of Appeal exists to remedy any wrongful convictions that occur amongst the appeals against conviction that appear before it. Yet the Court cannot defeat, any more than any other part of the criminal process can, the problem of uncertainty. Most importantly, it may dismiss appeals that should have been allowed, which gives rise to a severe risk of injustice. Yet, despite this, it is told by the Criminal Appeal Act that it is entitled to dismiss appeals that it thinks are safe. As such, there must be some conceptual floor of protection that the Court should be expected to provide to appellants. It has been argued that the concept of risk provides that floor; it should protect appellants from unacceptable risk, but it need not protect from all risk.

Whether the Court meets that baseline level of required protection was assessed in Chapter 3 of this book. It was argued there that most appellants, amongst the Court's routine decisions that largely disappear into the history of

1 R W Kates, C Hohenemser, J Kasperson, *Perilous Progress: Managing the Hazards of Technology* (Westview Press, 1985) 21.

the Court, do not come close to giving rise to an unacceptable risk of injustice. There is a degree of unreality in the assertion that the Court is in some manner generally unduly cautious in such circumstances. It is true that any appellant appearing before the Court of Appeal could in fact be innocent. Perpetuation of such an injustice is a significant wrong and it should be avoided wherever possible. Yet appellants, even the innocent, cannot realistically be expected to be protected from all risk. The examination of appeals against conviction discussed in Chapter 3 ultimately concluded that overall the Court does adequately perform its duties to protect from unacceptable risk, subject to a small number of problem areas.

The Law Commission's consultation into the criminal appeal system, and the likely publication of its final proposals in 2026, means that reform to the appeal system may be forthcoming in the future. It has been argued that if reform is directed towards correcting an allegedly unduly cautious approach, when arguably such an approach does not actually exist and certainly the Court does not accept what does not exist, would be futile and highly likely to fail. As a result, reform should be directed towards properly codifying the assessment of risk into the Court's decision-making processes. Chapter 4 of this book made suggestions as to how this could be done.

This book, therefore, provides a novel and timely appraisal of the criminal appeal system at a conceptual and also empirical level. Conceptually, it is crucial that the function of the Court is placed on a proper footing and that the Court is properly understood as a risk taking organisation. Empirically, understanding the Court as a risk taking organisation provides a baseline of what can be expected of the Court. In summary, the Court can only be expected to protect appellants from unacceptable risk, not from all risk. The evidence adduced in this book suggests that the Court does on the whole adequately fulfil that objective.

Conclusion

This book has offered an innovative way of viewing the Court of Appeal and its approach towards the unsafety test in appeals against conviction, through the lens of risk and risk assessment. Since there is the potential for reform to the Court's powers in the foreseeable future, it is crucial that the Court's function is placed on a secure footing so it can be assessed to what extent it properly performs its functions. From this lens, it has been argued that the Court's function is to protect appellants from unacceptable risk and that, overall, it does perform that function as required.

Reference

Kates, R W, Hohenemser, C, Kasperson, J, *Perilous Progress: Managing the Hazards of Technology* (Westview Press, 1985)

Bibliography

Allen, R J, Pardo, M S, 'Relative Plausibility and Its Critics' (2019) 23 *International Journal of Evidence and Proof* 5

Anon, 'Ill-treatment of a Patient' (2024) 10 *Archbold Review* 3

Appeal, Response to Law Commission Consultation (Appeal, 2025)

Associated Provincial Pictures Houses Ltd v Wednesbury Corp [1948] 1 KB 223

Atkins, B T S, 'Building a Lexicon: The Contribution of Lexicography' (1991) 4 (3) *International Journal of Lexicography* 167

Auld, R, *Review of the Criminal Courts of England and Wales* (HMSO, 2001)

Bar Standards Board, *Handbook* (BSB, 2026)

Benn, A, 'Causing a Public Nuisance' (2025) 1 *Criminal Law Review* 45

Bentham, J, *The Rationale of Punishment* (Robert Heward, 1830)

Biederman, A, Caruso, D, Kotsoglou, K N, 'Decision Theory, Relative Plausibility and the Criminal Standard of Proof' (2021) 15 *Criminal Law and Philosophy* 131

Bingham, T, *The Business of Judging* (Oxford University Press, 2000)

Boholm, M, Moller, N, Hansson, S O, 'The Concepts of Risk, Safety, and Security: Applications in Everyday Language' (2016) 36 (2) *Risk Analysis* 320

Bouder, F, Salvin, D, Lofstedt, R E, (eds), *The Tolerability of Risk: A New Framework for Risk Management* (Earthscan, 2007)

Boyle, T, *Health and Safety: Risk Management* (5th edn, Routledge, 2019)

Brewis, B, Dargue, P, 'Sexual Behaviour Evidence in the Court of Appeal (Criminal Division): Presenting the Need for Reform' (2025) 89 (6) *Journal of Criminal Law* 279

Chen, C, 'A Missed Opportunity to Correct the Law on Indecent Assault against Children' (2025) 89 (6) *Journal of Criminal Law* 349

Cohen, F E, 'Transcendental Nonsense and the Functional Approach' (1935) 35 (6) *Columbia Law Review* 809

Cohen, J, *An Introduction to the Philosophy of Induction and Probability* (Oxford University Press, 1989)

Commons Library, *Court Statistics for England and Wales* (2026)

Concise Oxford English Dictionary (11th edn, Oxford University Press, 2008)

Court of Appeal, *Annual Report 2019–2020*, https://www.judiciary.uk/wp-content/uploads/2022/07/6.7429_JO_Court_of_Appeal_Criminalwillbet.pdf

Court of Appeal, *Annual Report 2022–2023*, https://www.judiciary.uk/wp-content/uploads/2024/07/24.16_JO_A_Review_of_the_Year_In_the_Court_of_Appeal_Criminal_Division_2022-23_WEB.pdf

Court of Appeal, *Annual Report 2023–2024*, https://www.judiciary.uk/wp-content/uploads/2025/01/24.278_JO_A_Review_of_the_Year_In_the_Court_of_Appeal_Criminal_Division_2023-24_WEB.pdf
Courts Act 2003
Criminal Appeal Act 1907
Criminal Appeal Act 1964
Criminal Appeal Act 1966
Criminal Appeal Act 1968
Criminal Appeal Act 1995
Criminal Bar Association, Response to Law Commission Consultation (CBA, 2025)
Criminal Procedure Rules
Crown Court Compendium
Crown Prosecution Service, *Code for Crown Prosecutors* (CPS, 2026)
Dahlman, C, Stein, A, Tuzet, G, (eds), *Philosophical Foundations of Evidence Law* (Oxford University Press, 2021)
Darbyshire, P, *Sitting in Judgment: The Working Lives of Judges* (Hart, 2011)
Dargue, P, 'An Analysis of Disclosure Failings in Murder Appeals Against Conviction' (2020) *Criminal Law Review* 707
Dargue, P, 'The Safety of Convictions in the Court of Appeal: Fresh Evidence in the Criminal Division through an Empirical Lens' (2019) 83 (6) *Journal of Criminal Law* 433
Dargue, P, 'The Tolerability of Risk in the Court of Appeal (Criminal Division): An Empirical Study of Appeals against Conviction 2015–2021' (2025) *Criminal Law Review* 743
Dennis, I, *The Law of Evidence* (8th edn, Oxford University Press, 2024)
DPP v Rogers (1953) 37 Cr App R 137
European Convention on Human Rights
Fairclough v Whipp (1951) 35 Cr App R 138
Gillies, D, *Philosophical Theories of Probability* (Routledge, 2000)
Gross, S R, O'Brien, B, 'Frequency and Predictors of False Conviction: Why We Know So Little, and New Data on Capital Cases' (2008) 5 (4) *Journal of Empirical Legal Studies* 927
Hájek, A, 'The Reference Class Problem Is Your Problem Too' (2007) 156 (3) *Synthese* 563
Hart, H L A, (ed), *The Concept of Law* (3rd edn, Oxford University Press, 2012)
Hart, H L A, (ed), *Punishment and Responsibility* (2nd edn, Oxford University Press, 2008)
Hastie, R, Dawes, R M, *Rational Choice in an Uncertain World* (Sage, 2001)
Health and Safety at Work etc Act 1974
Heffer, C N, 'The Language of Conviction and the Convictions of Certainty: Is "Sure" an Impossible Standard of Proof?' (2007) 5 (1) *International Commentary on Evidence* i
Hillier, T, Dingwall, G, *Criminal Justice and the Pursuit of Truth* (Bristol University Press, 2021)
Home Office, *Papers Relating to the Case of George Edalji* (Cd. 3503, 1907)
HSE, *Reducing Risks, Protecting People: HSE Decision-Making Process* (HSE, 2001)
Huff, C R, Killias, M, (eds), *Wrongful Convictions and Miscarriages of Justice* (Routledge, 2013)

Human Rights Act 1998

Hungerford-Welch, P, 'Ill-Treatment of a Person in Care' (2025) 2 *Criminal Law Review* 102

Intelligence and Security Committee, *Report on the Intelligence Relating to the Murder of Fusilier Lee Rigby* (HC 795, 2014)

Judiciary of England and Wales, *The Court of Appeal Criminal Division Guide to Commencing Proceedings* (2021), https://www.judiciary.uk/wp-content/uploads/2021/07/Blue-guide-July-2021-Final-1.pdf

Judiciary of England and Wales, Guidance on Completing Form NG, https://assets.publishing.service.gov.uk/media/5fdb228d8fa8f54d60878b3b/ng-guidance.pdf

Justice, *Criminal Appeals* (Stevens and Sons, 1964)

Justice Committee 12th Report of Session 2014–15, *Criminal Cases Review Commission* (2015 HC 850)

Kates, R W, Hohenemser, C, Kasperson, J, *Perilous Progress: Managing the Hazards of Technology* (Westview Press, 1985)

Keane, A, 'Not So Sure About the Criminal Standard of Proof' (2020) 170 (7898) *New Law Journal* 15

Knight, M, *Criminal Appeals* (Stevens and Sons, 1970)

Law Commission, *Criminal Appeals: Consultation Paper* (Law Comm No 268, 2025)

Law Commission, *Criminal Appeals: Issues Paper* (Law Commission, 2023)

Law Society, Response to Law Commission Consultation (Law Society, 2025)

Lindley, DV, *Understanding Uncertainty, Revised Edition* (John Wiley & Sons, 2014)

Lord Chancellor's Office, Interdepartmental Committee on the Court of Criminal Appeal, *Report* (1965 Cmnd 2755)

Lützhöft, M, Oltedal, H, (eds), *Managing Maritime Safety* (Routledge, 2018)

Mackay, R, 'Fitness to Plead' (2024) 8 *Criminal Law Review* 576

Malleson, K, *The Royal Commission on Criminal Justice Research Study No 17* (HMSO, 1993)

McCartney, C, Roberts, S, 'Building Institutions to Address Miscarriages of Justice in England and Wales: "Mission Accomplished?"' (2013) 80 (4) *University of Cincinnati Law Review* 1333

McKay, C, 'Predicting Risk in Criminal Procedure: Actuarial Tools, Algorithms, AI, and Judicial Decision-Making' (2020) 32 (1) *Current Issues in Criminal Justice* 22

McKeown, P, 'The Crown Court Compendium and the Criminal Standard of Proof: Suggestions to aid Juror Comprehension and Help Judges' (2022) 11 *Criminal Law Review* 893

McKeown, P, Keane, A, Stares, S, 'Comprehension of "Sure" as the Description of the Criminal Standard of Proof: An Empirical Study' (2025) 9 *Criminal Law Review* 518

Miller v Minister of Pensions [1947] 2 All ER 372

Ministry of Justice, *Criminal Justice Statistics Quarterly September 2025* (MOJ 2025)

Ministry of Justice, *Root and Branch Review of the Parole System* (CP 654 2022)

Mullin, C, *Error of Judgment: The Truth about the Birmingham Bombings* (Poolbeg Press, 1990)

Murphy-Oikonen, J, McQueen, K, Miller, A, Chambers, L, 'Gatekeepers to Justice: Police Officers' Experiences Responding to Sexual Assault' (2024) 70 (12) *Crime and Delinquency* 3442
Naughton, M, *The Innocent and the Criminal Justice System: A Sociological Analysis of Miscarriages of Justice* (Palgrave MacMillan, 2013)
Nicholson, D, 'Taking Epistemology Seriously: "Truth, Reason and Justice" Revisited' (2013) 17 (1) *International Journal of Evidence and Proof* 1
Nobles, R, Schiff, D, 'The Never Ending Story: Disguising Tragic Choices in Criminal Justice' (1997) 60 (2) *Modern Law Review* 293
Nobles, R, Schiff, D, 'The Supervision of Guilty Pleas by the Court of Appeal of England and Wales – Workable Relationships and Tragic Choices' (2020) *Criminal Law Forum* 513
Nobles, R, Schiff, D, *Understanding Miscarriages of Justice: The Law, The Media, and the Inevitability of Crisis* (Oxford University Press, 2000)
Oberdiek, J, *Imposing Risk: A Normative Framework* (Oxford University Press, 2017)
Parl Deb HC 29 July 1907
Parole Board, *Types of Case Member Guidance* (Parole Board, 2023), https://www.gov.uk/government/publications/parole-board-types-of-cases-guidance-2023
Parpworth, N, 'Public Nuisance and the Meaning of a "Section of the Public"' (2025) 89 (1) *Journal of Criminal Law* 52
Pattenden, R, *English Criminal Appeals 1844–1994* (Clarendon Press, 1996)
Placani, A, Broadhead, S, (eds), *Risk and Responsibility in Context* (Routledge, 2024)
Police and Criminal Evidence Act 1984
R (On the Application of DSD) v Parole Board for England and Wales [2019] QB 285
R v:
AAB [2024] EWCA Crim 880
ADD and others [2022] EWCA Crim 106
Adebolajo; Adebowale [2014] EWCA Crim 2779
AFH [2024] EWCA Crim 1614 [29]
Ahmed [2010] EWCA Crim 2899
AJJ and others [2021] EWCA Crim 1278
Ali [2024] EWCA Crim 77
Allen (1909) 1 Cr App R 18
Al-Shumari [2025] EWCA Crim 1317
BAA [2024] EWCA Crim 343
Ben Smith [2024] EWCA Crim 342
BJK [2024] EWCA Crim 667
BJS [2024] EWCA Crim 1356
BNN [2024] EWCA Crim 991
BOB [2024] EWCA Crim 1494
Brooker [2024] EWCA Crim 103
Brown [2024] EWCA Crim 426
Burridge [2010] EWCA Crim 2847
BVY [2024] EWCA Crim 1355
Campbell [2024] EWCA Crim 1036

Cashman [2024] EWCA Crim 1543
Castree [2008] EWCA Crim 1866
CCRC ex parte Pearson [2000] 1 Cr App R 141
Cooper (1969) 53 Cr App R 82
Crane [2024] EWCA Crim 312
D [2013] EWCA Crim 1592
Davis, Rowe, and Johnson [2001] 1 Cr App R 8
Dundon [2004] EWCA Crim 621
Dunn [2015] EWCA Crim 724
Erskine [2009] EWCA Crim 1425
Essien [2024] EWCA Crim 598
Falcon [2024] EWCA Crim 311
FGH [2024] EWCA Crim 1353
Fisher [2024] EWCA Crim 1605
Gaiziunas [2024] EWCA Crim 246
Galbraith [2024] EWCA Crim 1148
H [2015] EWCA Crim 46
Hanna [2024] EWCA Crim 1315
Hanson and others [2005] EWCA Crim 824
Hayes [2015] EWCA Crim 1944
Hayes [2024] EWCA Crim 304
Hayes [2025] UKSC 29
Head [2024] EWCA Crim 1487
Heaven [2024] EWCA Crim 88
Hill [2024] EWCA Crim 1423
Horseferry Road Magistrates ex parte Bennett [1994] 1 AC 42
Hussain [2024] EWCA Crim 1223
Ismail [2024] EWCA Crim 301
Jodeiri-Lakpour [2024] EWCA Crim 97
Joshua Smith [2024] EWCA Crim 1040
Karim [2024] EWCA Crim 1773
Kent [2024] EWCA Crim 1271
Khan [2024] EWCA Crim 148
Kiszko (1979) 68 Cr App R 62
Kutek [2024] EWCA Crim 1675
Laws 1 Cr App R 6
Lee (1909) 1 Cr App R 5
Letby [2024] EWCA Crim 748
Letby [2024] EWCA Crim 1278
Lewis (1938) 26 Cr App R 110
LMS [2024] EWCA Crim 96
Lucas (1981) 73 Cr App R 159
Malkinson [2006] EWCA Crim 1891
Malkinson [2023] EWCA Crim 954
Mark Smith [2024] EWCA Crim 390
Matthew Banner; R v Peter Bennett [2024] EWCA Crim 1201
McIlkenny and others (1991) 93 Cr App R 28
McNaughton [2024] EWCA Crim 1129
Menzies [2024] EWCA Crim 1549
Mundle [2024] EWCA Crim 1289

N [2024] EWCA Crim 489
Oni [2024] EWCA Crim 893
Oni and others [2025] EWCA Crim 12
Osborne (1909) 1 Cr App R 144
P [2024] EWCA Crim 488
Pendleton [2001] UKHL 66
Peterkin [2024] EWCA Crim 309
Pope [2012] EWCA Crim 2241
Reid [2024] EWCA Crim 308
Reynolds [2024] EWCA Crim 317
Serdoud [2024] EWCA Crim 1398
Simpson (1909) 2 Cr App R 128
Somers [2024] EWCA Crim 1767
Stafford and Luvaglio [1974] AC 878
Tams [2024] EWCA Crim 582
Togher [2001] 3 All ER 463
TT [2024] EWCA Crim 616
W [2022] EWCA Crim 1438
Ward [2024] EWCA Crim 1696
Wills [2024] EWCA Crim 1351
Wilson [2024] EWCA Crim 1514
Winter [2024] EWCA Crim 711
Zulfiqar and others [2024] EWCA Crim 1710
Rawls, J, *A Theory of Justice Revised Edition* (Harvard University Press, 1999)
Re RS (Best Interests: Surgery and Intensive Care) [2025] EWCOP 38
Roberts, P, Zuckerman, A, *Roberts and Zuckerman's Criminal Evidence* (3rd edn, Oxford University Press, 2022)
Roberts, S, 'Fresh Evidence and Factual Innocence in the Criminal Division of the Court of Appeal' (2017) 81 (4) *Criminal Law Review* 304
Roberts, S, 'Reviewing the Function of the Criminal Appeals in England and Wales' (2017) 1 *Institute of Law Journal* 1
Ross, R E, *The Court of Criminal Appeal* (Butterwort and Co., 1911)
Royal Commission on Criminal Justice, *Report* (Cm 2263, 1993)
Seabourne Davies, D, 'The Court of Criminal Appeal: The First Forty Years' (1951) 1 *Journal of the Society of Public Teachers of Law* (N.S) 425
Sjolin, C, 'The Need to Kill Off Zombie Law: Indecent Assault, Where It Went Wrong and How to Put It Right' (2017) 81 *Journal of Criminal Law* 50
Smith, J, 'The Criminal Appeal Act 1995: Part 1: Appeals against Conviction' (1995) *Criminal Law Review* 920
Spencer, J R, 'Criminal Law and Criminal Appeals: The Tail that Wags the Dog?' (1982) *Criminal Law Review* 290
Spencer, J R, 'Quashing Convictions for Procedural Irregularities' (2007) *Criminal Law Review* 835
Stein, A, *Foundations of Evidence Law* (Oxford University Press, 2005)
Stephen, J, *A Digest on the Law of Evidence* (5th edn, 1887)
Tadros, V, *The Ends of Harm: The Moral Foundations of Criminal Law* (Oxford University Press, 2011)
Taylor, N, Ormerod, D, 'Mind the Gaps: Safety, Fairness, and Moral Legitimacy' (2004) *Criminal Law Review* 266
Taylor, P, *Taylor on Criminal Appeals* (3rd edn, Oxford University Press, 2022)

Trimpop, T M, *The Psychology of Risk Taking Behaviour* (Elsevier, 1994)
Twining, W, *Rethinking Evidence: Exploratory Essays* (2nd edn, Cambridge University Press, 2006)
Twining, W, 'Some Scepticism about Some Scepticisms' (1984) 11 *Journal of Law and Society* 137
UK Government, https://www.gov.uk/government/organisations/parole-board
UK Government, https://www.gov.uk/government/statistics/reported-road-casualties-great-britain-annual-report-2024/reported-road-casualties-great-britain-annual-report-2024#overall-casualties-and-rates
United States v Connolly and Black No. 19-3806
Wadham, J, Mountfield, H, Prochaska, E, Desai, R, *Blackstone's Guide to the Human Rights Act 1998* (7th edn, Oxford University Press, 2015)
Walker, C, Starmer, K, (eds), *Miscarriages of Justice: A Review of Justice in Error* (Oxford University Press, 1999)
Yates, J F, (ed), *Risk-Taking Behaviour* (John Wiley and Sons, 1992)
Zander, M, 'The Criminal Standard of Proof: How Sure Is Sure?' (2000) 150 (1517) *New Law Journal* 18

Index

For Product Safety Concerns and Information please contact our EU representative GPSR@taylorandfrancis.com Taylor & Francis Verlag GmbH, Kaufingerstraße 24, 80331 München, Germany